. . . the impact of the limerick, even at its most graphic, is on the intellect, not the genitals. It appeals to the alert, acute mind. The fun it creates springs from the intricacy of the rhyme scheme and the incongruity of the situation.

—L. T. Woodward, M.D.

this edition follows the text
of the 1953 Paris edition from
Les Hautes Etudes

THE LIMERICK

1700 EXAMPLES, WITH NOTES

VARIANTS AND INDEX

BOOK ONE

with an introduction by

L. T. WOODWARD, M.D.

THE LIMERICK

BOOK ONE

INTRODUCTION

By L. T. Woodward, M.D.

The publication of the book you now hold is something of an historic occasion. For just about a century, gifted English and American poets have devoted their ingenuity to what one critic, Brander Matthews, has called "the only original verse form of the English language"—the limerick. Yet up till now, virtually very important limerick written has seen public print either in a costly, difficult-to-obtain limited edition, or else in a bootlegged typed or mimeographed version available only to a very few. Now, for the first time, a unique treasury of this unique verse form is at last made accessible to the general reading public.

Why has the limerick been suppressed this way?

Because it is bawdy, is the obvious answer. Many limericks use "forbidden" words, blatant language, and too-picturesque imagery.

But the obvious answer is not the whole answer. In the case of the limerick, the truth lies in its satiric, devasting nature. The limerick is not merely bawdy; it is *cleverly* bawdy. It dares to make fun of sex, to poke a mocking finger into the puffed-up balloon of official dogma. No institution, no person, is safe from the sly shaft of the limerick-writer's art.

For example:

There was a young lady of Chichester
Who made all the saints in their niches stir.
One morning at matins
Her breast in white satins
Made the Bishop of Chichester's britches stir.

This example is limerick Number 540 from the text. A variant version is noted in the "Notes & Variants" section. Yet another variant, and one not included in this collection, is as follows:

There was a young girl from Chichester,
Who made all the saints in their niches stir.
As she wiggled her ass
While going to mass
She made the Bishop of Chichester's britches stir.

The foregoing is a highly typical example of the bawdy limerick, even though the final line is not strictly in the true limerick meter. These are its identifying characteristics:

1. It is a verse of five lines, of which the first, second, and fifth rhyme with one another, and the third and fourth rhyme with one another (A,A, B,B, A.)
2. Its meter is normally anapestic—that is, two short syllables followed by a long one: dee dee DAH, dee dee DAH, dee dee DAH. This is not always followed strictly, as we see above, but the essential beat of most lines has to be anapestic where some extra or missing syllables are found.
3. The first, second, and fifth lines have three accented syllables; the pair of inner lines has only two.
4. The rhymes are usually far-fetched: "Chichester" with

"britches stir."

5. There is a bawdy element: "As she wiggled her ass."
6. There is an element of satire: the suggestion that saints and bishops are capable of responding to the provocative wigglings of the girl in question.

That, basically, is the nature of the limerick. There are other minor characteristics, such as the custom of beginnig each limerick with the words, "There was . . ." In the nineteenth century nearly every specimen of the form started with that formula, but today's limerick writers try to avoid that stereotyped opening, as in this example (limerick Number 1473):

While Titian was mixing rose-madder,
His model posed nude on a ladder.
Her position, to Titian,
Suggested coition,
So he climbed up the ladder and had 'er.

A variant version, again not included in this text, goes as follows:

While Titian was mixing his madder
His model ascended a ladder
Her position to Titian
Suggested coition
So he went up the ladder and hadder.

Literary historians have expended a good deal of energy tracing the ancestry and evolution of the limerick back through the ages. It is generally agreed that the first authentic limericks, using the five-line form and the anapestic meter, were "nonsense rhymes," intended for children and published about 1820 in England. They have been traced to such children's books as *Anecdotes and Adventures of Fifteen Gentlewomen,* by one R. S. Sharpe, and *The History of Sixteen Wonderful Old Women.* There was nothing too offensive about these nursery jingles, naturally. This is a typical one from one of these collections:

There was a sick man of Tobago
Liv'd long on rice-gruel and sago;
But at last, to his bliss,
The physician said this—
"To a roast leg of mutton you may go."

The catchy rhythms and compact situation of the limerick failed to start a craze just then. It remained for a curious Englishman named Edward Lear to seize on the form and turn it into a fad a generation later.

Lear, like Lewis Carroll, was one of those odd Victorian gentlemen who never married, preferred the company of children to that of adults, and won considerable fame producing supposedly "nonsense" literature that actually contained a great deal of material of interest to psychoanalysts. (We could get very far off the track, let us say, by talking about the sexual symbolism in *Alice in Wonderland.*) About 1834, while serving as tutor to the family of the Earl of Derby, Lear came across the "sick man of Tobago" verse and began to compose dozens of new ones to amuse his pupils. These he collected and published in *The Book of Nonsense* in 1846.

The Edward Lear type of limerick differs in one major way both from the form that inspired it and from the bulk of the limericks that followed. Instead of creating a new fifth line to cap his limerick, Lear merely re-shaped his first line by way of climax—a lame and weak way to end the verse. Use of this formula allowed Lear to dash off hundreds of limericks without much effort, all of them free from overt offensiveness. Some of Lear's limericks were gently sly and silly, but a good many of them embodied a not-very-subtle sadism, violence, and sexual hostility. This limerick* demostrates both Lear's form of the limerick and Lear's hidden view of the relationship between the sexes in marriage:

There was an Old Man of Peru
Who watched his wife making a stew;
But once, by mistake,
In a stove she did bake
That unfortunate Man of Peru.

Lear did not call his jingles "limericks" at all, but simply "nonsense rhymes." The name "limerick" began to be attached to the form somewhere in the 1880's, and no one knows exactly why. Limerick is the name of a city and its surrounding county in Ireland, not far from the airport of Shannon. Supposedly a song whose chorus was, "Will you come up to limerick," was sung between rounds of verse at parties at which limericks were recited, but this theory has been greatly discredited by literary historians. Another idea—that verses of this kind were popular among the soldiers of the Irish Brigade who served in the French Army in the eighteenth century, and that it was the French who dubbed the verses "limericks"—does not really stand up to close inspection. The mystery of the origin of the name is nearly as deep as the mystery of the authorship of the great bawdy limericks.

The real limerick craze began in England in 1863, when Lear's *Book of Nonsense,* which had attained little attention in its first edition, was reissued. Suddenly everyone was quoting limericks. Lear, instantly famous, wrote hundreds more of the things. The humor magazine, *Punch,* sponsored limerick contests. New books of "nonsense rhymes" were produced by various hands. Educated men

---

*It is quite interesting to compare Lear's limerick with limerick Number 79 in this collection, and to speculate whether or not Number 79 is a true variant on Lear.

and women everywhere racked their brains for jingles beginning, "There was—"

Since this was the pious Victorian era, all of these new limericks, of course, were spotlessly pure and well suited to the amusement of the young. But puritanism always calls forth a more sordid sublevel; the repressed bawdiness merely goes underground and simmers and bubbles there. At the height of the limerick fad, about 1868, the editors of *Punch* were dismayed to discover that many of the rhymes submitted for the magazine's limerick contests were shockingly wicked. At once the contests were called off. But it was too late; the bawdy limerick as an art form was born, and from that day on the clean limerick was dead. Many of the triumphant jingles of this anti-fad are still in circulation; some are to be found in this book, as funny as ever after a century of going the rounds.

The "unprintable" limericks that began appearing at this time were quite frequently variations on the innocent, namby-pamby verses of Edward Lear. Given the right attitude of mind, it was not very hard to transform Lear's—

There was an Old Man of the Cape
Who buggered a Barbary ape.
Till the Ape, one dark night,
Set the house all alight,
Which burned that Old Man of the Cape.

into limerick Number 584 from this collection—

There was an old man of the Cape
Who buggered a Barbary ape.
The ape said, "You fool!
You've got a square tool;
You've buggered my arse out of shape."

or into yet another quite minor variation (not included herein)—

There was an old man of the Cape
Who buggered a Barbary ape.
Said the ape, "You old fool,
You've got a square tool,
And you've buggered my arse out of shape!"

Who composed the bawdy limericks?

Some of England's most highly respected poets were responsible. Good limericks were and are difficult things to write, requiring skill and a real gift of rhyme. In the England of the 1860's, the most gifted poet of all, technically speaking, was the saintly Algernon Charles Swinburne, whose lyrics delighted every maiden lady. In private life, Swinburne was addicted to a remarkable variety of vices, but of course he could not let any hint of his perversions creep into his acknowledged poetry if he wished to have it published. So to ease his private inclinations, Swinburne created some extravagantly funny, extravagantly bawdy limericks. He is usually credited with the ingenius one that begins:

There was a young couple of Aberystwyth
*Who united the organs they kissed with . . . .**

And many others. Another Victorian versifier who allegedly produced a host of bawdy limericks was the perfumed, oh-so-aesthetic Dante Gabriel Rossetti. W. S. Gilbert is supposed to have churned out limericks galore when not writing the libretti for *H.M.S. Pinafore* and *The Mikado.* In this country, Mark Twain contributed his share of unprintable bawdiness, as well as some of American poetry's biggest names. I can testify from personal

---

*A limerick oddly not included in the main part of this collection, however, do compare it with the very first limerick herein, as well as limerick Number 1071 and Note 1 under "Notes & Variants."

knowledge that a winner of the Pulitzer Prize for Poetry has devised some of the most sizzling limericks of modern times—his manuscript, in mimeographed or Xeroxed form, has been making the rounds of Ivy League schools for the past decade, to the amazement of delighted professors and the horrification of startled students.

Which brings us to an important point. The audience for bawdy limericks is a sophisticated, educated one. The verses are practically unknown among the working class, who prefer the more straightforward earthiness of the dirty joke or the long, explicitly blatant erotic ballad. It is impossible to imagine a group of construction workers sitting around over beer in a tavern after a hard day of digging ditches, telling each other limericks.

The reason seems to be that the impact of the limerick, even at its most graphic, is on the intellect, not the genitals. It appeals to the alert, acute mind. The fun it creates springs from the intricacy of the rhyme scheme and the incongruity of the situation. Such a limerick as this (Number 982 from this collection) invariably brings howls of pleasure in campus surroundings, but provokes only a blank stare of incomprehension among the uneducated:

There was a young lady named Sheba,
Fell in love with an eager amoeba.
This queer bit of jelly
Crept into her belly,
And ecstatically murmured, "Ich liebe!"

Or, to compare Number 982 to a variant version not included herein:

There was a young girl from Beersheba
Who was loved by a German amoeba.
As the Teutonic jelly
Slid down her belly
It quietly murmured, "Ich liebe."

The harshly unromantic tone of many limericks often offends those of lower education levels, too. Limerick Number 1008, for example:

There was a young lady from Cue
Who filled her vagina with glue.
She said with a grin,
"If they pay to get in,
They'll pay to get out of it too."

Or, comparing this with a new variant:

There once was a whore from Peru
Who filled her vagina with glue.
She said with a grin,
"You pay to get in,
And you'll pay to get out of it too."

Thus it is that the limerick is almost exclusively the plaything of the intellectual elite—an art form as fixed and stylized, and thus as rarefied in its appeal, as the seventeen-syllable *haiku* of Japan. And so we find professors of medieval literature painstakingly collecting limericks and writing learned commentaries on their origins; we find psychoanalysts studing the themes of limericks, examining not merely the cleverness of the way things are said, but the meaning of what is being said; and we find men of culture and refinement everywhere showing an unusual degree of interest in this seemingly humble five-line verse.

Tracing the pre-Lear limerick has been a task worthy of a doctorate in early English literature. G. Legman, an outstanding authority on erotic folklore, claims to see the beginnings of the limerick form—though not the meter—in the thirteenth century poem, "Sumer is i-cumen in," but this appears to me rather far-fetched:

Ewé bleateth after lamb,
Low'th after calvé coo;
Bullock starteth
Bucké farteth
Merry sing cuckoo!

What we have here is the framework of the five-line structure with the internal rhyme, but not much else of the limerick form is to be found here—except for the indelicate reference to the buck's behavior in the fourth line. That sets the tone for the future development of this verse form. As Legman points out, the limerick was always earthy and blunt, dealing with low matters of sex and bodily functions, throughout its centuries of development. Something about this particular rhythm and rhyme makes it peculiarly suitable for the bawdy, and the brief era of Edward Lear's non-bawdy limerick seems merely like an aberration against the larger background of cheeerful coarseness.

Various authorities have unearthed five-line pre-limericks in the literature of the fourteenth and fifteenth centuries. By the time we reach the Elizabethan era, we find many poets and playwrights employing the form. The anapestic meter, with its familiar jogging pace, has not yet emerged; but Shakespeare, Ben Jonson, Robert Herrick, and other men of that glorious epoch of letters made use of the iambic beat (a short syllable followed by a long) for their pre-limericks. There are half a dozen of them in Shakespeare, all of them drinking songs or else the raving of madmen—indicating that Shakespeare had come to regard this structure as best suited only for the bawdy. This sample is Iago's drinking song from *Othello:*

And let me the canikin clink, clink;
And let me the canikin clink:
A soldier's a man;
A life's but a span;
Why then let a soldier drink.

In the seventeenth century, the pre-limerick acquires another of its identifying characteristics: the use of a proper name as part of the rhyme scheme. This gives the rhymer great freedom, of course, since he can invent any name he pleases to fit his plan. In the *Roxburghe Ballads,* a collection of rhymes dating from before 1640, we find this tipsy exchange:

Good morrow, neighbor Gamble,
Come let you and I go ramble:
Last night I was shot
Through the brains with a pot
And now my stomach doth wamble ....

Gramercy, neighbor Jinkin
I see thou lovest no shrinking,
And I, for my part
From thee will not start
Come fill us a little more drink in.

We can see the anapestic meter beginning to slip into the scheme in such lines as "Come fill us a little more drink in." And the use of names like "Gamble" and "Jinkin" to pad out the rhyme structure foreshadows Swinburne's young couple of Aberystwyth, Lear's old man of Peru, and many another. Part of the fun of the limerick in its true form is to devise the most outlandish geographical references and work them in with improbable rhymes. The girl from Beersheba, who is loved by a German amoeba, fits into this spirit of fun. (And the German amoeba itself is an inspired creation! But of course it was necessary to make the amoeba German if it were going to tell the girl, "Ich liebe," and so the entire beautiful structure fits together tightly and symmetrically.)

Limericks have been used for social criticism, for wry comment on the relationship of the sexes, for expressions of inner feelings of anxiety and hostility, and—mainly—

for fun. They have long been prized by connoisseurs. Many of them, certainly, are in strikingly bad taste; but reasons of taste, as the courts have increasingly ruled in the last decade, are not enough to justify suppression of the printed word. So, now, finally, in this magnificent collection, we have a splendid array of uninhibited limericks, the fruit of a century of dedicated craftsmanship on the part of anonymous geniuses. There is, as the phrase goes, something here to offend everyone . . . but also something here to give delight to those mature enough and clever enough to appreciate this intricate, fascinating, and irreverent species of verse.

—L. T. WOODWARD, M.D.

CONTENTS

SOURCES

THIS is the largest collection of limericks ever published, erotic or otherwise. The seventeen hundred examples gathered here stem, about one-third, from some twenty printed sources dating from 1870 to 1952, most of which duplicate each other to a great extent. The rest are principally from three oral collections, made in Ann Arbor, Michigan (MS. 1938-1941), in Berkeley, California (1942-1947), and in New York (1941-1952). Almost no British materials after 1928 have been available. The chapter-titles are those of *Lapses in Limerick,* the Michigan collection. A chronological list of the sources used follows. Fuller details, and a few minor sources, will be found in the bibliography preceding the notes.

Variant lines, couplets and conclusions are given at the end of the text, with varia in geographical and personal names (in rhyming positions) cited and indexed. Minor variations in phrasing and vocabulary have not seemed worth reporting here. A full Index, of names and rhymes, will be found at the end of the volume, and should make convenient the locating of any desired limerick in spite of the division of the text into chapters. A few folklore parallels are made and explanations given, but humorous and didactic excursi on the style of Norman Douglas' *Some Limericks* (1928) have not been attempted.

Sources are given for each limerick by means of the date. Dates and sources are listed together facing the next page. Where two dates follow a limerick, the second is the actual source of the text; the first is the earliest known variant printing or collecting of it.

These dates have other uses as well, such as turning up all the new limericks in any listed source, or the complete contents of the three known collections of original limericks: *Cythera's Hymnal* (1870), *The Pearl* (1879-1880), and *That Immoral Garland* (MS. 1942A). Chronological changes in the dominant limerick themes over the last eighty years in England and America may also easily be traced, and will provide an unparalleled key to the socio-sexual anxieties of the period.

No improvement has been made upon orally transmitted or printed materials. The limericks are given as found in the sources credited. (Exceptions: punctuation and the spelling of geographical names have been made uniform, expurgations have been spelled out, and the first names of real private persons have been dropped.) The text is eclectic only to the degree of choosing one form — not necessarily the oldest — on which to base all variants. The prejudices, cruelty, and humorless quality of many of the limericks included are deeply regretted. However, no falsification of the material has been made.

THE EDITOR.

SOURCES

1870. *Cythera's Hymnal, or Flakes from the Foreskin.*
1879 to 1880. *The Pearl* ('Oxford').
1882. *The Cremorne* ('March 1851').
1910 to 1911. Dr. SUSRUTA, in *Anthropophyteia.*
1927. *Immortalia* (Philadelphia).
1927A. *Anecdota Americana* ('Boston').
1928. Norman DOUGLAS: *Some Limericks.*
1928A. 'O. U. SCHWEINICKLE': *The Book of* 1000 *Laughs*
1928B. *Poems, Ballads and Parodies* ('Paris, 1923').
1928C. 'Dave E. JONES': *A Collection of Sea Songs.*
1932. 'John FALMOUTH': *Ninety-five Limericks.*
1934. *Anecdota Americana, Second Series* ('Boston').
1938 to 1941. *Lapses in Limerick* (MS.)
1939A. Weston LA BARRE, in *Psychiatry* (May 1939).
1941A. *Pornographia Literaria* (mimeo).
1942 to 1947. *Index Limericus* (MS.)
1942A. *That Immoral Garland* (MS.)
1943A. *Unexpurgated* (Los Angeles).
1943B. [Clement WOOD] *The Facts of Life in Limericks.*
1943C. *An Investigation into... Limericks* (mimeo).
1944A to 1948A. New York (oral collection).
1945C. *Farmer Gray* (mimeo).
1946B. [DAVIS] *The International Set.*
1947B. [HARRISON MS.]
1948. [MORSE] *The Limerick: A Facet of Our Culture.*
1949. [DRAKE] *A Book of Anglo-Saxon Verse.*
1950 to 1952. New York (oral collection).

I

LITTLE ROMANCES

1

There was a young girl of Aberystwyth
Who took grain to the mill to get grist with.
    The miller's son, Jack,
    Laid her flat on her back,
And united the organs they pissed with.

1927-1941.

2

There was a young lady of Arden,
The tool of whose swain wouldn't harden.
    Said she with a frown,
  " I've been sadly let down
By the tool of a fool in a garden."

1941.

3

There once was a yokel of Beaconsfield
Engaged to look after the deacon's field,
    But he lurked in the ditches
    And diddled the bitches
Who happened to cross that antique 'un's field.

1941.

4

There's a charming young lady named Beaulieu
Who's often been screwed by yours truly,
    But now—it's appallin'—
    My balls always fall in!
I fear that I've fucked her unduly.

1941.

5

There was a young girl in Berlin
Who was fucked by an elderly Finn.
    Though he diddled his best,
    And fucked her with zest,
She kept asking, "Hey, Pop, is it in?"

1927-1941.

6

I wooed a stewed nude in Bermuda,
I was lewd, but my God! she was lewder.
    She said it was crude
    To be wooed in the nude—
I pursued her, subdued her, and screwed her!

1941-1952.

7

There was a young lady of Bicester
Who was nicer by far than her sister:
    The sister would giggle
    And wiggle and jiggle,
But this one would come if you kissed her.

1941-1952.

8

There once was a son-of-a-bitch,
Neither clever, nor handsome, nor rich,
    Yet the girls he would dazzle,
    And fuck to a frazzle,
And then *ditch* them, the son-of-a-bitch!

1941.

9

There was a young fellow named Blaine,
And he screwed some disgusting old jane.
    She was ugly and smelly,
    With an awful pot-belly,
But... well, they were caught in the rain.

1941.

10

There was a young sailor from Brighton
Who remarked to his girl, " You're a tight one."
She replied, " 'Pon my soul,
You're in the wrong hole;
There's plenty of room in the right one."

1882-1943C.

11

A lacklustre lady of Brougham
Weaveth all night at her loom.
Anon she doth blench
When her lord and his wench
Pull a chain in the neighbouring room.

1942.

12

A middle-aged codger named Bruin
Found his love life completely a-ruin,
For he flirted with flirts
Wearing pants and no skirts,
And he never got in for no screwin'.

1946A.

13

There was a young fellow of Burma
Whose betrothed had good reason to murmur.
But now that he's married he's
Been using cantharides
And the root of their love is much firmer.

1939A.

14

There was a young fellow from Cal.,
In bed with a passionate gal.
He leapt from the bed,
To the toilet he sped;
Said the gal, " What about *me*, old pal? "

1952.

15

There was a young man from Calcutta
Who was heard in his beard to mutter,
  " If her Bartholin glands
    Don't respond to my hands,
I'm afraid I shall have to use butter. "

1947B.

16

There once was a kiddie named Carr
Caught a man on top of his mar.
    As he saw him stick 'er,
    He said with a snicker,
" You do it much faster than par. "

1927.

17

There was a young fellow named Charteris
Put his hand where his young lady's garter is.
    Said she, " I don't mind,
    And up higher you'll find
The place where my fucker and farter is. "

1927-1941.

18

A young woman got married at Chester,
Her mother she kissed and she blessed her.
    Says she, " You're in luck,
    He's a stunning good fuck,
For I've had him myself down in Leicester. "

1870.

19

" For the tenth time, dull Daphnis, " said Chloe,
" You have told me my bosom is snowy;
    You have made much fine verse on
    Each part of my person,
Now *do* something—there's a good boy! "

1942.

20

A maiden who wrote of big cities
Some songs full of love, fun and pities,
Sold her stuff at the shop
Of a musical wop
Who played with her soft little titties.

1935*

21

There once was a gouty old colonel
Who grew glum when the weather grew vernal,
And he cried in his tiffin
For his prick wouldn't stiffen,
And the *size* of the thing was infernal.

1941.

22

A lady while dining at Crewe
Found an elephant's whang in her stew.
Said the waiter, " Don't shout,
And don't wave it about,
Or the others will all want one too. "

1941.

23

There was a young lady of Dee
Who went down to the river to pee.
A man in a punt
Put his hand on her cunt,
And God! how I wish it was me.

1870-1941.

24

I never have had Miss Defauw,
But it wouldn't have been quite so raw
If she'd only said " No "
When I wanted her so;
But she didn't—she laughed and said " Naw! "

1941.

25

A beautiful belle of Del Norte
Is reckoned disdainful and haughrty
    Because during the day
    She says : " Boys, keep away! "
But she fucks in the gloaming like forty.

1946A.

26

A young man by a girl was desired
To give her the thrills she required,
    But he died of old age
    Ere his cock could assuage
The volcanic desire it inspired.

1941.

27

There was a young lady of Dover
Whose passion was such that it drove her
    To cry, when you came,
    " Oh dear! What a shame!
Well, now we shall have to start over. "

1941.

28

There was a young man of Dumfries
Who said to his girl, " If you please,
    It would give me great bliss
    If, while playing with this,
You would pay some attention to these! "

1941.

29

There was a young lady of Ealing
And her lover before her was kneeling.
    Said she, " Dearest Jim,
    Take your hand off my quim;
I much prefer fucking to feeling. "

1870.

30

A lonely young lad of Eton
Used always to sleep with the heat on,
Till he ran into a lass
Who showed him her ass—
Now they sleep with only a sheet on.

1943.

31

There was a young lady of Exeter,
So pretty, that men craned their necks at her.
One was even so brave
As to take out and wave
The distinguishing mark of his sex at her.

1927-1941.

32

There was a young lady of fashion
Who had oodles and oodles of passion.
To her lover she said,
As they climbed into bed,
" Here's *one* thing the bastards can't ration! "

1942.

33

There was a young girl in Dakota
Had a letter from Ickes; he wrote her:
" In addition to gas
We are rationing ass,
And you've greatly exceeded your quota. "

1942.

34

There was a young lady named Flynn
Who thought fornication a sin,
But when she was tight
It seemed quite all right,
So everyone filled her with gin.

1927-1941.

35

A reckless young lady of France
Had no qualms about taking a chance,
But she thought it was crude
To get screwed in the nude,
So she always went home with damp pants.

1941.

36

A nervous young fellow named Fred
Took a charming young widow to bed.
When he'd diddled a while
She remarked with a smile,
" You've got it all in but the head. "

1941.

37

There was a young fellow named Fyfe
Whose marriage was ruined for life,
For he had an aversion
To every perversion,
And only liked fucking his wife.

Well, one year the poor woman struck,
And she wept, and she cursed at her luck,
And said, " Where have you gotten us
With your goddamn monotonous
Fuck after fuck after fuck?

" I once knew a harlot named Lou—
And a versatile girl she was, too.
After ten years of whoredom
She perished of boredom
When she married a jackass like you! "

1938.

40

There was a young lady of Gloucester,
Met a passionate fellow who tossed her.
    She wasn't much hurt,
    But he dirtied her skirt,
So think of the anguish it cost her.

1927-1941.

41

There was a young lady of Gloucester
Whose friends they thought they had lost her,
    Till they found on the grass
    The marks of her arse,
And the knees of the man who had crossed her.

1870.

42

There was a young fellow named Goody
Who claimed that he wouldn't, but would he?
    If he found himself nude
    With a gal in the mood,
The question's not woody but could he?

1944A.

43

In my sweet little Alice Blue gown
Was the first time I ever laid down,
    I was both proud and shy
    As he opened his fly
And the moment I saw it I thought I would die.

Oh it hung almost down to the ground,
As it went in I made not a sound,
    The more that he shoved it
    The more that I loved it,
As he came on my Alice Blue gown.

1944A.

45

In my sweet little night gown of blue,
On the first night that I slept with you,
    I was both shy and scared
    As the bed was prepared,
And you played peekaboo with my ribbons of blue.

As we both watched the break of the day,
And in peaceful submission I lay,
    You said you adored it
    But dammit, you tore it,
My sweet little night gown of blue.

1944*

47

Winter is here with his grouch,
The time when you sneeze and slouch.
    You can't take your women
    Canoein' or swimmin',
But a lot can be done on a couch.

1927.

48

It always delights me at Hanks
To walk up the old river banks.
    One time in the grass
    I stepped on an ass,
And heard a young girl murmur, " Thanks. "

1946A.

49

There was a young girl from Hong Kong
Who said, " You are utterly wrong
    To say my vagina
    's the largest in China,
Just because of your mean little dong. "

1944.

50

There was once a sad Maître d'hôtel
Who said, " They can all go to hell!
What they do to my wife—
Why it ruins my life;
And the worst is, they all do it well."

1943A.

51

There was a young man named Hughes
Who swore off all kinds of booze.
He said, " When I'm muddled
My senses get fuddled,
And I pass up too many screws."

1927.

52

There were three ladies of Huxham,
And whenever we meets 'em we fucks 'em,
And when that game grows stale
We sits on a rail,
And pulls out our pricks and they sucks 'em.

1870.

53

There was a young lady named Inge
Who went on a binge with a dinge.
Now I won't breathe a word
Of what really occurred—
But her cunt has a chocolate fringe.

1943B.

54

An octogenarian Jew
To his wife remained steadfastly true.
This was not from compunction,
But due to dysfunction
Of his spermatic glands—nuts to you.

1941.

55

" Snyder's got a stiff ticket, " said Kay,
" Come on, take it out, and let's play. "
He pulled it on out,
But she started to pout,
His ticket was only a quarter-inch stout.

1943.

56

A pansy who lived in Khartoum
Took a lesbian up to his room,
And they argued all night
Over who had the right
To do what, and with which, and to whom.

1941-1952.

57

There was an old lady who lay
With her legs wide apart in the hay,
Then, calling the ploughman,
She said, " Do it now, man!
Don't wait till your hair has turned gray. "

1928-1941.

58

There was a young lady of Lee
Who scrambled up into a tree,
When she got there
Her arsehole was bare,
And so was her KUNT.

1870.

59

A worn-out young husband named Lehr
Heard daily his wife's plaintive prayer:
" Slip on a sheath, quick,
Then slip your big dick
Between these lips covered with hair. "

1945A.

60

There was a young plumber of Leigh
Who was plumbing a girl by the sea.
    She said, " Stop your plumbing,
    There's somebody coming! "
Said the plumber, still plumbing, " It's me. "

1927-1928.

61

Il y avait un plombier, François,
Qui plombait sa femme dans le Bois.
    Dit-elle, " Arrêtez!
    J'entends quelqu'un venait. "
Dit le plombier, en plombant, " C'est moi. "

1941.

62

Es giebt ein Arbeiter von Tinz,
Er schläft mit ein Mädel von Linz.
    Sie sagt, " Halt sein' plummen,
    Ich höre Mann kommen. "
" Jacht, jacht, " sagt der Plummer, " Ich binz. "

1952.

63

Prope mare erat tubulator
Qui virginem ingrediebatur.
    Dessine ingressus
    Audivi progressus :
Est mihi inquit tubulator.

1941.

64

Have you heard of knock-kneed Samuel McGuzzum
Who married Samantha, his bow-legged cousin ?
    Some people say
    Love finds a way,
But for Sam and Samantha it doesn'.

1947B.

65

In bed Dr. Oscar McPugh
Spoke of Spengler—and ate crackers too.
His wife said, " Oh, stuff
That philosophy guff
Up your ass, dear, and throw me a screw! "

1941.

66

There was a young lady named Maud
A terrible society fraud :
In company, I'm told
She was awfully cold.
But if you got her alone, Oh God!

1927.

67

There was a young lady named May
Who strolled in a park by the way,
And she met a young man
Who fucked her and ran—
Now she goes to the park every day.

1941.

68

There once was a Swede in Minneapolis,
Discovered his sex life was hapless :
The more he would screw
The more he'd want *to,*
And he feared he would soon be quite sapless.

1946A.

69

There was a young dolly named Molly
Who thought that to frig was folly.
Said she, " Your pee-pee
Means nothing to me,
But I'll do it just to be jolly. "

1927.

70

Of his face she thought *not* very much,
But then, at the very first touch,
Her attitude shifted—
He was terribly gifted
At frigging and fucking and such.

1948A.

71

The King plugged the Queen's ass with mustard
To make her fuck hot, but got flustered,
And he cried, " Oh, my dear,
I am coming, I fear,
But the mustard will make you come *plus tard!* "

1941.

72

There was a young lad from Nahant
Who was made like the Sensitive Plant.
When asked, " Do you fuck? "
He replied, " No such luck.
I would if I could but I can't. "

1928-1932.

73

There was a young man of Natal
Who was fucking a Hottentot gal.
Said she, " You're a sluggard! "
Said he, " You be buggered!
I like to fuck slow, and I shall. "

1879-1941.

74

There was a young man of Natal
And Sue was the name of his gal.
One day, north of Aden,
He got his hard rod in,
And came clear up Suez Canal.

1928-1943B.

75

There was a gay dog from Ontario
Who fancied himself a Lothario.
At a wench's glance
He'd snatch off his pants
And make for her Mons Venerio.

1946A.

76

There was a young man of Ostend
Who let a girl play with his end.
She took hold of Rover,
And felt it all over,
And it did what she didn't intend.

1927-1941.

77

There was a young man of Ostend
Whose wife caught him fucking her friend.
" It's no use, my duck,
Interrupting our fuck,
For I'm damned if I draw till I spend. "

1879.

78

There was a young fellow from Parma
Who was solemnly screwing his charmer.
Said the damsel, demure,
" You'll excuse me, I'm sure,
But I *must* say you fuck like a farmer. "

1941.

79

A newly-wed man of Peru
Found himself in a terrible stew:
His wife was in bed
Much deader than dead,
And so he had no one to screw.

1946A.

80

There was a young girl of Pitlochry
Who was had by a man in a rockery.
    She said, " Oh! You've come
    All over my bum;
This isn't a fuck—it's a mockery."

1928.

81

There was a young lady named Prentice
Who had an affair with a dentist.
    To make the thing easier
    He used anesthesia,
And diddled her, *non compos mentis.*

1941.

82

There was a young man with a prick
Which into his wife he would stick
    Every morning and night
    If it stood up all right—
Not a very remarkable trick.

His wife had a nice little cunt:
It was hairy, and soft, and in front,
    And with this she would fuck him,
    Though sometimes she'd suck him—
A charming, if commonplace, stunt.

1941.

84

There was a young man from Purdue
Who was only just learning to screw,
    But he hadn't the knack,
    And he got too far back—
In the right church, but in the wrong pew.

1941.

85

A young lady sat on a quay,
Just as proper as proper could be.
  A young fellow goosed her,
  And roughly seduced her,
So she thanked him and went home to tea.

1941.

86

I once was annoyed by a queer
Who made his intentions quite clear.
  Said I, " I'm no prude,
  So don't think me rude,
But I'm already stewed, screwed, and tattooed. "

1944-1952.

87

A young wife in the outskirts of Reims
Preferred frigging to going to mass.
  Said her husband, " Take Jacques,
  Or any young cock,
For I cannot live up to your ass. "

1942A.

88

The king named Œdipus Rex
Who started this fuss about sex
  Put the world to great pains
  By the spots and the stains
Which he made on his mother's pubex.

1946A.

89

Now hear this fair lass from Rhode Isle
Who said with a wink and a smile,
  " Sure, please stick it in,
  Be it thick be it thin,
But if's rough I won't do as a file. "

1952.

90

There was a young lady of Rhyll
In an omnibus was taken ill,
So she called the conductor,
Who got in and fucked her,
Which did her more good than a pill.

1870.

91

There was a young German named Ringer
Who was screwing an opera singer.
Said he with a grin,
" Well, I've sure got it in! "
Said she, " You mean that ain't your finger? "

1941.

92

A young violinist from Rio
Was seducing a lady named Cleo.
As she took down her panties
She said, " No *andantes*;
I want this *allegro con brio!* "

1941.

93

A young Juliet of St. Louis
On a balcony stood, acting screwy.
Her Romeo climbed,
But he wasn't well timed,
And half-way up, off he went—blooey!

1927-1941.

94

Said a lecherous fellow named Shea,
When his prick wouldn't rise for a lay,
" You must seize it, and squeeze it,
And tease it, and please it,
For Rome wasn't built in a day. "

1941.

95

There was a young man from Siam
Who said, " I go in with a wham,
    But I soon lose my starch
    Like the mad month of March,
And the lion comes out like a lamb. "

1947.

96

Prince Absalom lay with his sister
And bundled and nibbled and kissed her,
    But the kid was so tight,
    And it was deep night—
Though he shot at the target, he missed her.

1942A.

97*

There was a young fellow named Skinner
Who took a young lady to dinner.
    At a quarter to nine
    They sat down to dine;
At twenty to ten it was in her.
    The dinner, not Skinner—
Skinner was in her before dinner.

There was a young fellow named Tupper
Who took a young lady to supper.
    At a quarter to nine
    They sat down to dine,
And at twenty to ten it was up her.
    Not the supper—not Tupper—
It was some son-of-a-bitch named Skinner!

1911-1948A.

99

" My back aches. My penis is sore.
I simply can't fuck any more.
    I'm dripping with sweat,
    And you haven't come yet;
And, my God! it's a quarter to four! "

1941.

100

There was a young lady of Spain
Who took down her pants on a train.
    There was a young porter
    Saw more than he orter,
And asked her to do it again.

1939A.

101

There was a young man of high station
Who was found by a pious relation
    Making love in a ditch
    To—I won't say a bitch—
But a woman of *no* reputation.

1938.

102

There once was a dentist named Stone
Who saw all his patients alone.
    In a fit of depravity
    He filled the wrong cavity,
And my, how his practice has grown!

1945-1947B.

103

A sailor who slept in the sun
Woke to find his fly-buttons undone.
    He remarked with a smile,
    "Jesus Christ, a sundial!
And it's now a quarter past one."

1948A.

104

A plumber whose name was Ten Brink
Plumbed the cook as she bent o'er the sink.
    Her resistance was stout,
    And Ten Brink petered out
With his pipe-wrench all limber and pink.

1942A.

105

The spouse of a pretty young thing
Came home from the wars in the spring.
He was lame but he came
With his dame like a flame—
A discharge is a wonderful thing.

1947B.

106

I wonder what my wife will want tonight;
Wonder if the wife will fuss and fight?
I wonder can she tell
That I've been raising hell;
Wonder if she'll know that I've been tight?

My wife is just as nice as nice can be,
I hope she doesn't feel too nice toward me,
For an afternoon of joy
Is hell on the old boy.
I wonder what the wife will want tonight!

1927.

108

There's an unbroken babe from Toronto,
Exceedingly hard to get onto,
But when you get there,
And have parted the hair,
You can fuck her as much as you want to.

1941.

109

Une jolie épousette à Tours
Voulait de gig-gig tous les jours.
Mais le mari disait, « Non!
De trop n'est pas bon!
Mon derrière exige du secours! »

1942A.

110

A pretty wife living in Tours
Demanded her daily amour.
But the husband said, "No!
It's too much. Let it go!
My backsides are dragging the floor."

1942A.

111

In the shade of the old apple tree
Where between her fat legs I could see
A little brown spot
With the hair in a knot,
And it certainly looked good to me.

I asked as I tickled her tit
If she thought that my big thing would fit.
She said it would do
So we had a good screw
In the shade of the old apple tree.

In the shade of the old apple tree
I got all that was coming to me.
In the soft dewy grass
I had a fine piece of ass
From a maiden that was fine to see.

I could hear the dull buzz of the bee
As he sunk his grub hooks into me.
Her ass it was fine
But you should have seen mine
In the shade of the old apple tree.

1928B.

115

A lad from far-off Transvaal
Was lustful, but tactful withal.
    He'd say, just for luck,
  " Mam'selle, do you fuck? "
But he'd bow till he almost would crawl.

1939A.

116

There was a young lady of Twickenham
Who thought men had not enough prick in 'em
    On her knees every day
    To God she would pray
To lengthen and strengthen and thicken 'em.

1927-1932.

117

There was a young lady named Twiss
Who said she thought fucking a bliss,
    For it tickled her bum
    And caused her to come
While comfortably lying like this.

1948A.

118

There once was a husky young Viking
Whose sexual prowess was striking.
    Every time he got hot
    He would scour the twat
Of some girl that might be to his liking.

1947.

119

At the moment Japan declared war
A sailor was fucking a whore.
    He said, " After this poke
    'Long and hard' ain't no joke;
This means *months* till I get back ashore. "

1942-1951.

120

There was a young lady of Wheeling
Said to her beau, " I've a feeling
My little brown jug
Has need of a plug "—
And straightway she started to peeling.

1927.

121

Two anglers were fishing off Wight
And his bobber was dipping all night.
Murmured she, with a laugh,
" It is ready to gaff,
But don't break your rod, which is light. "

A couple was fishing near Clombe
When the maid began looking quite glum,
And said, " Bother the fish!
I'd rather coish! "
Which they did—which was why they had come.

As two consular clerks in Madras
Fished, hidden in deep shore-grass,
" What a marvelous pole, "
Said she, " but control
Your sinkers—they're banging my ass. "

1942A.

124

Love letters no longer they write us,
To their homes they so seldom invite us.
It grieves me to say,
They have learned with dismay,
We can't cure their *vulva pruritus.*

1927.

125

There was a young student from Yale
Who was getting his first piece of tail.
    He shoved in his pole,
    But in the wrong hole,
And a voice from beneath yelled : " No sale! "

1941.

II

ORGANS

126

In the Garden of Eden lay Adam,
Complacently stroking his madam,
    And loud was his mirth
    For on all of the earth
There were only two balls—and he had 'em.

1941.

127

There was a young bride of Antigua
Whose husband said, " Dear me, how big you are! "
    Said the girl, " What damn'd rot!
    Why, you've often felt my twot,
My legs and my arse and my figua! "

1880.

128

There was a young damsel named Baker
Who was poked in a pew by a Quaker.
    He yelled, " My God! what
    Do you call this—a twat?
Why, the entrance is more than an acre! "

1943B.

129

There was once a mechanic named Bench
Whose best tool was a sturdy gut-wrench.
    With this vibrant device
    He could reach, in a trice,
The innermost parts of a wench.

1943A.

130

There was a young man of Bengal
Who swore he had only one ball,
But two little bitches
Unbuttoned his britches,
And found he had *no* balls at all.

1870-1941.

131

A chippy who worked in Black Bluff
Had a pussy as large as a muff.
It had room for both hands
And some intimate glands,
And was soft as a little duck's fluff.

1942A.

132

There was a young lady named Blount
Who had a rectangular cunt.
She learned for diversion
Posterior perversion,
Since no one could fit her in front.

1943A.

133

There was a young fellow named Bowen
Whose pecker kept growin' and growin'.
It grew so tremendous,
So long and so pendulous,
'Twas no good for fuckin'—just showin'.

1945C.

134

There was a young lady named Brent
With a cunt of enormous extent,
And so deep and so wide,
The acoustics inside
Were so good you could hear when you spent.

1941.

135

There was a young girl from the Bronix
Who had a vagina of onyx.
She had so much *tsoris*
With her clitoris,
She traded it in for a Packard.

1943C.

136

There was a young lady from Brussels
Who was proud of her vaginal muscles.
She could easily plex them
And so interflex them
As to whistle love songs through her bustles.

1941A-1942.

137

There was a young lady of Bude
Who walked down the street in the nude.
A bobby said, " Whattum
Magnificent bottom! "
And slapped it as hard as he could.

1938.

138

There once was a Queen of Bulgaria
Whose bush had grown hairier and hairier,
Till a Prince from Peru
Who came up for a screw
Had to hunt for her cunt with a terrier.

1938.

139

There was a young girl of Cah'lina,
Had a very capricious vagina:
To the shock of the fucker
'Twould suddenly pucker,
And whistle the chorus of " Dinah."

1941.

140

A lady with features cherubic
Was famed for her area pubic.
When they asked her its size
She replied in surprise,
" Are you speaking of square feet, or cubic ? "

1941.

141

There was a fat lady of China
Who'd a really enormous vagina,
And when she was dead
They painted it red,
And used it for docking a liner.

1941.

142

I met a young man in Chungking
Who had a very long thing—
But you'll guess my surprise
When I found that its size
Just measured a third-finger ring!

1945.

143

There was a young man of Coblenz
Whose ballocks were simply immense :
It took forty-four draymen,
A priest and three laymen
To carry them thither and thence.

1941.

144

There was an old man of Connaught
Whose prick was remarkably short.
When he got into bed
The old woman said,
" This isn't a prick, it's a wart. "

1879.

145

There once was a girl from Cornell
Whose teats were shaped like a bell.
When you touched them they shrunk,
Except when she was drunk,
And then they got bigger than hell.

1939A.

146

There once was a lady of Crete
So enormously broad in the beam
That one day in the ocean
She caused such commotion
That Admiral Byrd claimed her for America.

1946A.

147

There was a young fellow named Cribbs
Whose cock was so big it had ribs.
They were inches apart,
And to suck it took art,
While to fuck it took forty-two trips.

1944-1951.

148

There was a young lady whose cunt
Could accomodate a small punt.
Her mother said, " Annie,
It matches your fanny,
Which never was that of a runt."

1941*

149

There's a young Yiddish slut with two cunts,
Whose pleasure in life is to pruntz.
When one pireg is shot,
There's that alternate twat,
But the ausgefuckt male merely grunts.

1941.

150

There was a young man from Dallas
Who had an exceptional phallus.
He couldn't find room
In any girl's womb
Without rubbing it first with Vitalis.

1946A.

151

There was a young girl of Des Moines
Whose cunt could be fitted with coins,
Till a guy from Hoboken
Went and dropped in a token,
And now she rides free on the ferry.

1948A.

152

To his bride said the keen-eyed detective,
"Can it be that my eyesight's defective?
Has the east tit the least bit
The best of the west tit,
Or is it the faulty perspective?"

1941-1942.

153

There was a young girl of Detroit
Who at fucking was very adroit:
She could squeeze her vagina
To a pin-point, or finer,
Or open it out like a quoit.

1926*

And she had a friend named Durand
Whose cock could contract or expand.
He could diddle a midge
Or the arch of a bridge—
Their performance together was grand!

1938.

155

There was a young man of Devizes
Whose balls were of different sizes.
His tool, when at ease,
Hung down to his knees,
Oh, what must it be when it rises!

1927-1941.

156

Visas erat: huic geminarum
Dispar modus testicularum:
Minor haec nihili,
Palma triplici,
Jam fecerat altera clarum.

1941.

157

There was a young fellow whose dong
Was prodigiously massive and long.
On each side of this whang
Two testes did hang
That attracted a curious throng.

1942.

158

There was a young man from East Wubley
Whose cock was bifurcated doubly.
Each quadruplicate shaft
Had two balls hanging aft,
And the general effect was quite lovely.

1947-1951.

159

While I, with my usual enthusiasm,
Was exploring in Ermintrude's busiasm,
She explained, "They are flat,
But think nothing of that—
You will find that my sweet sister Susiasm."

1943.

160

There was a young fellow from Florida
Who liked a friend's wife, so he borrowed her.
When they got into bed
He cried, "God strike me dead!
This ain't a cunt—it's a corridor!"

1927-1941.

161

An old man at the Folies Bergère
Had a jock, a most wondrous affair:
It snipped off a twat-curl
From each new chorus girl,
And he had a wig made of the hair.

1942A.

162

There was a young man with one foot
Who had a very long root.
If he used this peg
As an extra leg
Is a question exceedingly moot.

1939*

163

In the case of a lady named Frost,
Whose cunt's a good two feet acrost,
It's the best part of valor
To bugger the gal, or
You're apt to fall in and get lost.

1941.

164

A certain young person of Ghent,
Uncertain if lady or gent,
Shows his organs at large
For a small handling charge
To assist him in paying the rent.

1944A.

165

There was an old woman of Ghent
Who swore that her cunt had no scent.
She got fucked so often
At last she got rotten,
And didn't she stink when she spent.

1870.

166

There was a young man from Glengozzle
Who found a remarkable fossil.
He knew by the bend
And the wart on the end,
'Twas the peter of Paul the Apostle.

1938.

167

There was a young fellow of Greenwich
Whose balls were all covered with spinach.
He had such a tool
It was wound on a spool,
And he reeled it out inich by inich.

But this tale has an unhappy finich,
For due to the sand in the spinach
His ballocks grew rough
And wrecked his wife's muff,
And scratched up her thatch in the scrimmage.

1927-1941.

169

A mathematician named Hall
Had a hexahedronical ball,
And the cube of its weight
Times his pecker, plus eight,
Was four fifths of five eighths of fuck-all.

1941.

170

There was a young fellow of Harrow
Whose john was the size of a marrow.
He said to his tart,
" How's this for a start?
My balls are outside in a barrow."

1941.

171

There was a young fellow named Harry,
Had a joint that was long, huge and scary.
He pressed it on a virgin
Who, without any urgin',
Immediately spread like a fairy.

1943.

172

There was a young girl named Heather
Whose twitcher was made out of leather.
She made a queer noise,
Which attracted the boys,
By flapping the edges together.

1945c.

173

There was an old curate of Hestion
Who'd erect at the slightest suggestion.
But so small was his tool
He could scarce screw a spool,
And a cunt was quite out of the question.

1941.

174

There was a young man from Hong Kong
Who had a trifurcated prong:
A small one for sucking,
A large one for fucking,
And a *honey* for beating a gong.

1942.

175

A fellow whose surname was Hunt
Trained his cock to perform a slick stunt:
    This versatile spout
    Could be turned inside out,
Like a glove,-and be used as a cunt.

1942.

176

Alas for the Countess d'Isère,
Whose muff wasn't furnished with hair.
    Said the Count, "Quelle surprise!"
    When he parted her thighs;
"Magnifique! Pourtant pas de la guerre."

1941.

177

A highly aesthetic young Jew
Had eyes of a heavenly blue;
    The end of his dillie
    Was shaped like a lily,
And his balls were too utterly *two*!

1941.

178

There once was a lady from Kansas
Whose cunt was as big as Bonanzas.
    It was nine inches deep
    And the sides were quite steep—
It had whiskers like General Carranza's.

1927-1932.

179

Oh, pity the Duchess of Kent!
Her cunt is so dreadfully bent,
    The poor wench doth stammer,
    "I need a sledgehammer
To pound a man into my vent."

1939A.

180

There was an old gent from Kentuck
Who boasted a filigreed schmuck,
But he put it away
For fear that one day
He might put it in and get stuck.

1952.

181

There was an old lady of Kewry
Whose cunt was a *lusus naturæ* :
The *introitus vaginæ*
Was unnaturally tiny,
And the thought of it filled her with fury.

1941.

182

There was a young fellow named Kimble
Whose prick was exceedingly nimble,
But fragile and slender,
And dainty and tender,
So he kept it encased in a thimble.

1941.

183

There was a young man of Lahore
Whose prick was one inch and no more.
It was all right for key-holes
And little girls' pee-holes,
But not worth a damn with a whore.

1927-1941.

184

There once was a horse named Lily
Whose dingus was really a dilly.
It was vaginoid duply,
And labial quadruply—
In fact, he was really a filly.

1942-1952.

185

There was a young fellow from Leeds
Who swallowed a package of seeds.
    Great tufts of grass
    Sprouted out of his ass
And his balls were all covered with weeds.

1938-1952.

186

The wife of young Richard of Limerick
Complained to her husband, "My quim, Rick,
    Still grows in diameter
    Each time that you ram at her;
How can your poor tool stay so slim, Rick?"

1944.

187

There was a young lady of Lincoln
Who said that her cunt was a pink'un,
    So she had a prick lent her
    Which turned it magenta,
This artful old lady of Lincoln.

1870.

188

There was a young girl of Llewellyn
Whose breasts were as big as a melon.
    They were big, it is true,
    But her cunt was big too,
Like a bifocal, full-color, aerial view
Of Cape Horn and the Straits of Magellan.

1941.

189

A contortionist hailing from Lynch
Used to rent out his tool by the inch.
    A foot cost a quid—
    He could and he did
Stretch it to three in a pinch.

1942A.

190

There was a young man from Lynn
Whose cock was the size of a pin.
    Said his girl with a laugh
    As she felt his staff,
" This won't be much of a sin. "

1927.

191

There was a young girl named McCall
Whose cunt was exceedingly small,
    But the size of her anus
    Was something quite heinous—
It could hold seven pricks and one ball.

1941.

192

There was an old satyr named Mack
Whose prick had a left-handed tack.
    If the ladies he loves
    Don't spin when he shoves,
Their cervixes frequently crack.

1950.

193

An envious girl named McMeanus
Was jealous of her lover's big penis.
    It was small consolation
    That the rest of the nation
Of women were with her in weeness.

1942-1952.

194

There was a young man named McNamiter
With a tool of prodigious diameter.
    But it wasn't the size
    Gave the girls a surprise,
But his rhythm—iambic pentameter.

1946A.

195

There was a young man of Madras
Whose balls were constructed of brass.
Whe.. jangled together
They played " Stormy Weather, "
And lightning shot out of his ass.

1938.

196

A bad little girl in Madrid,
A most reprehensible kid,
Told her Tante Louise
That her cunt smelled like cheese,
And the worst of it was that it did!

1941.

197

There was a young man from Maine
Whose prick was as strong as a cane;
It was almost as long,
So he strolled with his dong
Extended in sunshine and rain.

1952.

198

There was a young girl from Medina
Who could completely control her vagina.
She could twist it around
Like the cunts that are found
In Japan, Manchukuo and China.

1948.

199

There was a young fellow named Morgan
Who possessed an unusual organ:
The end of his dong,
Which was nine inches long,
Was tipped with the head of a gorgon.

1943A.

200

There was a young soldier from Munich
Whose penis hung down past his tunic,
And their chops girls would lick
When they thought of his prick,
But alas! he was only a eunuch.

1941.

201

There was a young lady of Natchez
Who chanced to be born with two snatches,
And she often said, " Shit!
Why, I'd give either tit
For a man with equipment that matches."

There was a young fellow named Locke
Who was born with a two-headed cock.
When he'd fondle the thing
It would rise up and sing
An antiphonal chorus by Bach.

But whether these two ever met
Has not been recorded as yet,
Still, it would be diverting
To see him inserting
His whang while it sang a duet.

1939*-1941.

204

A girl of uncertain nativity
Had an ass of extreme sensitivity
When she sat on the lap
Of a German or Jap,
She could sense Fifth Column activity.

1943B-1946A.

205

There was a gay parson of Norton
Whose prick, although thick, was a short 'un.
To make up for this loss,
He had balls like a horse,
And never spent less than a quartern.

1879.

206

A farmer I know named O'Doole
Has a long and incredible tool.
He can use it to plow,
Or to diddle a cow,
Or just as a cue-stick at pool.

1946A.

207

A chap down in Oklahoma
Had a cock that could sing La Paloma,
But the sweetness of pitch
Couldn't put off the hitch
Of impotence, size and aroma.

1952.

208

There was a young girl named O'Malley
Who wanted to dance in the ballet.
She got roars of applause
When she kicked off her drawers,
But her hair and her bush didn't tally.

1941.

209

There was a young maiden from Osset
Whose quim was nine inches across it.
Said a young man named Tong,
With tool nine inches long,
"I'll put bugger-in if I loss it."

1942.

210

" The testes are cooler outside, "
Said the doc to the curious bride,
" For the semen must not
Get too fucking hot,
And the bag fans your bum on the ride. "

1942A.

211

There was a young fellow named Paul
Who confessed, " I have only one ball.
But the size of my prick
Is God's dirtiest trick,
For my girls always ask, 'Is that all?' "

1943A-1952.

212

There was a young girl of Pawtucket
Whose box was as big as a bucket.
Her boy-friend said, " Toots,
I'll have to wear boots,
For I see I must muck it, not fuck it. "

1941.

213

When I was a baby, my penis
Was as white as the buttocks of Venus.
But now 'tis as red
As her nipples instead—
All because of the feminine genus!

1939A.

214

Two roosters in one of our pens
Found their pricks were no larger than wens.
As they looked at their foreskins
And wished they had more skins,
They discovered they'd both become hens.

1941*

215

There was a young fellow of Perth
Whose balls were the finest on earth.
They grew to such size
That one won a prize,
And goodness knows what they were worth.

1941.

216

To his bride a young bridegroom said, "Pish!
Your cunt is as big as a dish!"
She replied, "Why, you fool,
With your limp little tool
It's like driving a nail with a fish!"

1941.

217

A very odd pair are the Pitts :
His balls are as large as her tits,
Her tits are as large
As an invasion barge—
Neither knows how the other cohabits.

1944-1951.

218

A young man from the banks of the Po
Found his cock had elongated so,
That when he'd pee
It was not he
But only his neighbors who'd know.

1944.

219

There was a young fellow named Prynne
Whose prick was so short and so thin,
His wife found she needed
A Fuckoscope—she did—
To see if he'd gotten it in.

1941.

220

A beautiful lady named Psyche
Is loved by a fellow named Ikey.
One thing about Ike
The lady can't like
Is his prick, which is dreadfully spikey.

1946A.

221

There was a fat man from Rangoon
Whose prick was much like a balloon.
He tried hard to ride her
And when finally inside her
She thought she was pregnant too soon.

1942.

222

There was a young fellow called Rex
With diminutive organs of sex.
When charged with exposure
He said with composure,
"*De minimis non curat lex!*"

1948-1952.

223

There was a young lady named Riddle
Who had an untouchable middle.
She had many friends
Because of her ends,
Since it isn't the middle you diddle.

1943A.

224

There was a young man from Salinas
Who had an extremely long penis:
Believe it or not,
When he lay on his cot
It reached from Marín to Martinez.

1942.

225

There was a young harlot named Schwartz
Whose cock-pit was studded with warts,
And they tickled so nice
She drew a high price
From the studs at the summer resorts.

Her pimp, a young fellow named Biddle,
Was seldom hard up for a diddle,
For according to rumor
His tool had a tumor
And a fine row of warts down the middle.

Her brother, a bastard named Ben,
Could rotate his pecker, and then
He would shoot through his rear
Which made him the dear
Of the girls, and the envy of men.

Her other young brother, named Saul,
Was able to bounce either ball,
He could stretch them and snap them,
And juggle and clap them,
Which earned him the plaudits of all.

1941.

229

The skater, Barbara Ann Scott
Is so fuckingly " winsome " a snot,
That when posed on her toes
She elaborately shows
Teeth, fat ass, titties and twat.

1952.

230

A cowhand way out in Seattle
Had a dooflicker flat as a paddle.
He said, " No, I can't fuck
A lamb or a duck,
But golly! it just fits the cattle. "

1941.

231

There was a young man from Seattle
Whose testicles tended to rattle.
He said as he fuckèd
Some stones in a bucket,
" If Stravinsky won't deafen you—that'll. "

1939A.

232

There's a lovely young lady named Shittlecock
Who loves to play diddle and fiddle-cock,
But her cunt's got a pucker
That's best not to fuck, or
When least you expect it to, it'll lock.

1952.

233

There was an old fellow named Skinner
Whose prick, his wife said, had grown thinner.
But still, by and large,
It would always discharge
Once he could just get it in her.

1941-1948.

234

An ingenious young man in South Bend
Made a synthetic arse for a friend,
But the friend shortly found
Its construction unsound,
It was simply a bother—no end.

1944A.

235

An aesthete from South Carolina
Had a cock that tinkled like china,
But while shooting his load
It cracked like old Spode,
So he's bought him a Steuben vagina.

1952.

236

There was a young blade from South Greece
Whose bush did so greatly increase
That before he could shack
He must hunt needle in stack.
'Twas as bad as being obese.

1944-1951.

237

There was a young lady from Spain
Whose face was exceedingly plain,
But her cunt had a pucker
That made the men fuck her,
Again, and again, and again.

1927A.

238

Il y avait une madame de Lahore
Dont la figure n'était la meilleure,
Mais la vagine très forte,
Toujours ouverte la porte,
Encore, et encore, et encore.

1941.

239

De Hispanice puella verumque
Simplex oris verborumque
Tulit potens vagina
Hominum agmina
Iterum iterum iterumque.

1941.

240

There once was a girl from Spokane
Went to bed with a one-legged man.
She said, " I know you—
You've really got two!
Why didn't you say so when we began? "

1942.

241

There was a young man from Stamboul
Who boasted so torrid a tool
That each female crater
Explored by this satyr
Seemed almost unpleasantly cool.

1939A.

242

There was a young fellow of Strensall
Whose prick was as sharp as a pencil.
On the night of his wedding
It went through the bedding,
And shattered the chamber utensil.

So here was this fellow of Strensall
Whose pecker was shaped like a pencil,
Anemic, 'tis true,
But an interesting screw,
Inasmuch as the tip was prehensile.

1938-1952.

244

A wonderful tribe are the Sweenies,
Renowned for the length of their peenies.
The hair on their balls
Sweeps the floors of their halls,
But they don't look at women, the meanies.

1943A.

245

There was an old man of Tagore
Whose tool was a yard long or more,
So he wore the damn thing
In a surgical sling
To keep it from wiping the floor.

1941.

246

There was a young lady whose thighs,
When spread showed a slit of such size,
And so deep and so wide,
You could play cards inside—
Much to her bridegroom's surprise.

1941.

247

There was a young hayseed from Tiffan
Whose cock would constantly stiffen.
This knob out in front
Attracted foul cunt
Which he greatly delighted in sniffin'.

1941*

248

There's a charming young girl in Tobruk
Who refers to her quiff as a nook.
It's deep and it's wide,
—You can curl up inside
With a nice easy chair and a book.

1946B.

249

There was a gay parson of Tooting
Whose roe he was frequently shooting,
Till he married a lass
With a face like my arse,
And a cunt you could put a top-boot in.

1879.

250

There was a young man of Toulouse
Who had a deficient prepuce,
But the foreskin he lacked
He made up in his sac;
The result was, his balls were too loose.

1943.

251

A wide-bottomed girl named Trasket
Had a hole as big as a basket.
A spot, as a bride,
In it now, you could hide,
And include with your luggage your mascot.

1946A.

252

A young man maintained that his trigger
Was so big that there weren't any bigger.
But this long and thick pud
Was so heavy it could
Scarcely lift up its head. It lacked vigor.

1941*

253

A cautious young fellow named Tunney
Had a whang that was worth any money.
When eased in half-way,
The girl's sigh made him say,
" Why the sigh? " " For the rest of it, honey. "

1942.

254

There was an old man who said, " Tush!
My balls always hang in the brush,
And I fumble about,
Half in and half out,
With a pecker as limber as mush. "

1941.

255

A pious old woman named Tweak
Had taught her vagina to speak.
It was frequently liable
To quote from the Bible,
But when fucking—not even a squeak!

1941.

256

There once was a newspaper vendor,
A person of dubious gender.
He would charge one-and-two
For permission to view
His remarkable double pudenda.

1941.

257

A maiden who lived in Virginny
Had a cunt that could bark, neigh and whinny.
The horsey set rushed her,
But success finally crushed her
For her tone soon became harsh and tinny.

1952.

258

There was a young fellow of Warwick
Who had reason for feeling euphoric,
For he could by election
Have triune erection:
Ionic, Corinthian, Doric.

1945-1949.

259

When he tried to inject his huge whanger
A young man aroused his girl's anger.
As they strove in the dark
She was heard to remark,
" What you need is a zeppelin hangar."

1942.

260

There was a young squaw of Wohunt
Who possessed a collapsible cunt.
 It had many odd uses,
 Produced no papooses,
And fitted both giant and runt.

1944A.

261

There was a young laundress named Wrangle
Whose tits tilted up at an angle.
 " They may tickle my chin, "
 She said with a grin,
" But at least they keep out of the mangle. "

1945.

262

An organist playing in York
Had a prick that could hold a small fork,
 And between obbligatos
 He'd munch at tomatoes,
And keep up his strength while at work.

1942A.

263

There was a young man named Zerubbabel
Who had only one real, and one rubber ball.
 When they asked if his pleasure
 Was only half measure,
He replied, " That is highly improbable. "

1941.

264

There was a young man named Zerubbabub
Who belonged to the Block, Fuck & Bugger Club;
 But the pride of his life
 Were the tits of his wife—
One real, and one India-rubber bub.

1941.

III

STRANGE INTERCOURSE

265

Thus spake I AM THAT I AM :
" For the Virgin I don't give a damn.
  What pleases Me most
  Is to bugger the Ghost,
And then be sucked off by the Lamb. "

1928.

266

Así dije YO SOY QUE YO SOY :
" Por La Vírgen un carajo no doy.
  Lo que debe gustar
  Es Jesús caporar—
Y para hacerlo Yo voy. "

1941.

267

Dame Catherine of Ashton-on-Lynches
Got on with her grooms and her wenches :
  She went down on the gents,
  And pronged the girls' vents
With a clitoris reaching six inches.

1942A.

268

There was a young lady named Astor
Who never let any get past her.
  She finally got plenty
  By stopping twenty,
Which certainly ought to last her.

1942.

269

Oden the bardling averred
His muse was the bum of a bird,
    And his Lesbian wife
    Would finger his fife
While Fisherwood waited as third.

1942A.

270

There was a young fellow named Babbitt
Who could screw nine times like a rabbit,
    But a girl from Johore
    Could do it twice more,
Which was just enough extra to crab it.

1942.

271

A young polo-player of Berkeley
Made love to his sweetheart berserkly.
    In the midst of each chukker
    He would break off and fuck her
Horizontally, laterally, and verkeley.

1943.

272

There once was a jolly old bloke
Who picked up a girl for a poke.
    He took down her pants,
    Fucked her into a trance,
And then shit in her shoe for a joke.

1941.

273

There was a young idler named Blood,
Made a fortune performing at stud,
    With a fifteen-inch peter,
    A double-beat metre,
And a load like the Biblical Flood.

1941.

274

Though the invalid Saint of Brac
Lay all of his life on his back,
His wife got her share,
And the pilgrims now stare
At the scene, in his shrine, on a plaque.

1943.

275

There was an old man of Brienz
The length of whose cock was immense:
With one swerve he could plug
A boy's bottom in Zug,
And a kitchen-maid's cunt in Coblenz.

1928.

276

There once was a Duchess of Bruges
Whose cunt was incredibly huge.
Said the King to this dame
As he thunderously came:
"Mon Dieu! Après moi, le déluge!"

1941.

277

There was an old man of Cajon
Who never could get a good bone.
With the aid of a gland
It grew simply grand;
Now his wife cannot leave it alone.

1941*

278

There was a young girl of Cape Cod
Who dreamt she'd been buggered by God.
But it wasn't Jehovah
That turned the girl over,
'Twas Roger the lodger, the dirty old codger,
The bugger, the bastard, the sod!

1938-1952.

279

There once was a lady named Carter,
Fell in love with a virile young Tartar.
She stripped off his pants,
At his prick quickly glanced,
And cried : " For that I'll be a martyr! "

1946A.

280

A talented fuckstress, Miss Chisholm,
Was renowned for her fine paroxysm.
While the man detumesced
She still spent on with zest,
Her rapture sheer anachronism.

1941.

281

There was a young man in the choir
Whose penis rose higher and higher,
Till it reached such a height
It was quite out of sight—
But of course you know I'm a liar.

1946A.

282

There was a young man from the Coast
Who had an affair with a ghost.
At the height of orgasm
Said the pallid phantasm,
" I think I can feel it—almost! "

1942.

283

Have you heard of the lady named Cox
Who had a capacious old box?
When her lover was in place
She said, " Please turn your face.
I look like a gal, but I screw like a fox. "

1942.

284

A team playing baseball in Dallas
Called the umpire a shit out of malice.
While this worthy had fits
The team made eight hits
And a girl in the bleachers named Alice.

1946A.

285

There was a young girl of Darjeeling
Who could dance with such exquisite feeling
There was never a sound
For miles around
Save of fly-buttons hitting the ceiling.

1943A-1949.

286

There was a young woman in Dee
Who stayed with each man she did see.
When it came to a test
She wished to be best,
And practice makes perfect, you see.

1927.

287

There was a family named Doe,
An ideal family to know.
As father screwed mother,
She said, "You're heavier than brother."
And he said, "Yes, Sis told me so!"

1948.

288

A lady, by passion deluded,
Found an African drunk and denuded,
And—fit as a fiddle,
And hot for a diddle—
She tied splints to his penis and screwed it.

1941.

289

There was a strong man of Drumrig
Who one day did seven times frig.
He buggered three sailors,
Four Jews and two tailors,
And ended by fucking a pig.

1879.

290

There was an old man of Duluth
Whose cock was shot off in his youth.
He fucked with his nose
And with fingers and toes,
And he came through a hole in his tooth.

1941.

291

There was an old man of Dundee
Who came home as drunk as could be.
He wound up the clock
With the end of his cock,
And buggered his wife with the key.

1927-1928.

292

A rapturous young fellatrix
One day was at work on five pricks.
With an unholy cry
She whipped out her glass eye:
" Tell the boys I can now take on six. "

1942-1952.

293

There was a young man with a fiddle
Who asked of his girl, " Do you diddle? "
She replied, " Yes, I do,
But prefer to with two—
It's twice as much fun in the middle. "

1943A.

294

I dined with Lord Hughing Fitz-Bluing
Who said, "Do you squirm when you're screwing?"
I replied, "Simple shagging
Without any wagging
Is only for screwing canoeing."

1947.

295

There was a young fellow named Fletcher,
Was reputed an infamous lecher.
When he'd take on a whore
She'd need a rebore,
And they'd carry him out on a stretcher.

1943A.

296

A young fellow discovered through Freud
That although of a penis devoid,
He could practice coitus
By eating a fœtus,
And his parents were quite overjoyed.

1941.

297

There was a young man from Jodhpur
Who found he could easily cure
His dread diabetes
By eating a fœtus
Served up in a sauce of manure.

1945.

298

There once was a sailor named Gasted,
A swell guy, as long as he lasted,
He could jerk himself off
In a basket, aloft,
Or a breeches-buoy swung from the masthead.

1941.

299

There was a young girl of Gibraltar
Who was raped as she knelt at the altar.
    It really seems odd
    That a virtuous God
Should answer her prayers and assault her.

1943A.

300

A young man with passions quite gingery
Tore a hole in his sister's best lingerie.
    He slapped her behind
    And made up his mind
To add incest to insult and injury.

1941*-1947B.

301

A passionate red-headed girl,
When you kissed her, her senses would whirl,
    And her twat would get wet
    And would wiggle and fret,
And her cunt-lips would curl and unfurl.

1941.

302

There was a young lady named Gloria
Who was had by Sir Gerald Du Maurier,
    And then by six men,
    Sir Gerald again,
And the band at the Waldorf-Astoria.

1943.

303

Thank God for the Duchess of Gloucester,
She obliges all who accost her.
    She welcomes the prick
    Of Tom, Harry or Dick,
Or Baldwin, or even Lord Astor.

1939A.

304

The latest reports from Good Hope
State that apes there have pricks thick as rope,
And fuck high, wide, and free,
From the top of one tree
To the top of the next—what a scope!

1941.

305

A newlywed couple from Goshen
Spent their honeymoon sailing the ocean.
In twenty-eight days
They got laid eighty ways—
Imagine such fucking devotion!

1941.

306

There was a young fellow named Grimes
Who fucked his girl seventeen times
In the course of a week—
And this isn't to speak
Of assorted venereal crimes.

1947.

307

There was a young lady named Hatch
Who would always come through in a scratch.
If a guy wouldn't neck her,
She'd grab up his pecker
And shove the damn thing up her snatch.

1945.

308

There was a young lady named Hilda
Who went for a walk with a builder.
He knew that he could,
And he should, and he would—
And he did—and he goddam near killed her!

1928A-1941.

309

Cum Hilde autem ambulabat
Homo qui ædificabat.
Dixit volebat. Debet et potebat.
Sic ille ducebat. Statim faciebat.
Sed virginem pine necebat.

1941.

310

I know of a fortunate Hindu
Who is sought in the towns that he's been to
By the ladies he knows,
Who are thrilled to the toes
By the tricks he can make his foreskin do.

1948A.

311

If you're speaking of actions immoral
Then how about giving the laurel
To doughty Queen Esther,
No three men could best her—
One fore, and one aft, and one oral.

1941-1952.

312

There was a young miss from Johore
Who'd lie on a mat on the floor;
In a manner uncanny
She'd wobble her fanny,
And drain your nuts dry to the core.

1942.

313

There was a young fellow of Kent
Whose prick was so long that it bent,
So to save himself trouble
He put it in double,
And instead of coming he went.

1927-1941.

314

There was a young man of Kildare
Who was fucking a girl on the stair.
  The bannister broke,
  But he doubled his stroke
And finished her off in mid-air.

1927-1952.

315

A young man of Llanfairpwllgwyngyll
While bent over plucking a dingle
  Had the whole Eisteddfod
  Taking turns at his pod
While they sang some impossible jingle.

1952.

316

There once were two brothers named Luntz
Who buggered each other at once.
  When asked to account
  For this intricate mount,
They said, " Ass-holes are tighter than cunts. "

1941.

317

There was a young lady named Mable
Who liked to sprawl out on the table,
  Then cry to her man,
  " Stuff in all you can—
Get your ballocks in, too, if you're able. "

1943.

318

An impotent Scot named MacDougall
Had to husband his sperm and be frugal.
  He was gathering semen
  To gender a he-man,
By screwing his wife through a bugle.

1941.

319

There once was a girl named McGoffin
Who was diddled amazingly often.
She was rogered by scores
Who'd been turned down by whores,
And was finally screwed in her coffin.

1941.

320

A stout Gaelic warrior, McPherson,
Was having a captive, a person
Who was not averse
Though she had the curse,
And he'd breeches of bristling furs on.

1942A.

321

There was a young Scot in Madrid
Who got fifty-five fucks for a quid.
When they said, " Are you faint? "
He replied, " No, I ain't,
But I *don't* feel as good as I did. "

1941.

322

There was a young fellow of Mayence
Who fucked his own arse, in defiance
Not only of custom
And morals, dad-bust him,
But most of the known laws of science.

1949.

323

The woman who lives on the moon
Is still cherishing the balloon
Of an earthling who'd come
And given her some,
But had dribbled away all too soon.

1942A.

324

There is a young faggot named Mose
Who insists that you fuck his long nose.
And you'll double the joy
Of this lecherous boy
If you'll tickle his balls with your toes.

1946A.

325

There was an Old Man of the Mountain
Who frigged himself into a fountain
Fifteen times had he spent,
Still he wasn't content,
He simply got tired of the counting.

1879.

326

There was a young lady named Nance
Who learned about fucking in France,
And when you'd insert it
She'd squeeze till she hurt it,
And shoved it right back in your pants.

1951.

327

A studious professor named Nestor
Bet a whore all his books he could best her.
But she drained out his balls
And skipped up the walls,
Beseeching poor Nestor to rest her.

1941A.

328

The late Brigham Young was no neuter—
No faggot, no fairy, no fruiter.
Where ten thousand virgins
Succumbed to his urgin's
There now stands the great State of Utah.

1941.

329

There was a young girl of Newcastle
Whose charms were declared universal.
  While one man in front
  Wired into her cunt,
Another was engaged at her arsehole.

1879.

330

There was a young girl from New York
Who plugged up her cunt with a cork.
  A woodpecker or two
  Made the grade, it is true,
But it totally baffled the stork.

Till along came a man who presented
A tool that was strangely indented.
  With a dizzying twirl
  He punctured that girl,
And thus was the cork-screw invented.

1938.

332

There was a young girl named O'Clare
Whose body was covered with hair.
  It was really quite fun
  To probe with one's gun,
For her quimmy might be anywhere.

1947.

333

There once was a gay young Parisian
Who screwed an appendix incision,
  And the girl of his choice
  Could hardly rejoice
At this horrible lack of precision.

1941.

334

While spending the winter at Pau
Lady Pamela forgot to say " No. "
 So the head-porter made her
 The second-cook laid her;
The waiters were all hanging low.

1942A.

335

There was a young girl of Penzance
Who boarded a bus in a trance.
 The passengers fucked her,
 Likewise the conductor.
The driver shot off in his pants.

1927-1928.

336

The Shah of the Empire of Persia
Lay for days in a sexual merger.
 When the nautch asked the Shah,
 " Won't you ever withdraw ? "
He replied with a yawn, " It's inertia. "

1938-1941.

337

A remarkable race are the Persians,
They have such peculiar diversions.
 They screw the whole day
 In the regular way,
And save up the nights for perversions.

1941.

338

There was a young girl of Rangoon
Who was blocked by the Man in the Moon.
 " Well, it *has* been great fun, "
 She remarked when he'd done,
" But I'm sorry you came quite so soon. "

1928-1941.

339

There was a young lady named Ransom
Who was rogered three times in a hansom.
When she cried out for more
A voice from the floor
Said, " My name is Simpson, not Samson. "

1938-1941.

340

A maestro directing in Rome
Had a quaint way of driving it home.
Whoever he climbed
Had to keep her tail timed
To the beat of his old metronome.

1942A.

341

" Last night, " said a lassie named Ruth,
" In a long-distance telephone booth,
I enjoyed the perfection
Of an ideal connection—
I was screwed, if you must know the truth."

1943A.

342

Said a Lesbian lady, " It's sad;
Of all of the girls that I've had,
None gave me the thrill
Of real rapture until
I learned how to be a tribade. "

1952.

343

There once was a handsome young seaman
Who with ladies was really a demon.
In peace or in war,
At sea or on shore,
He could certainly dish out the semen.

1942.

344

Said a girl being had in a shanty,
" My dear, you have got it in slanty."
  He replied, " I can use
  Any angle I choose.
I ride as I please—I'm Duranty!"

1939A.

345

An old couple just at Shrovetide
Were having a piece—when he died.
  The wife for a week
  Sat tight on his peak,
And bounced up and down as she cried.

1942A.

346

My wife is an amorous soul
On fire for an African's pole.
  She told a coon chauffeur
  That he was her gopher—
And, say, did he go for her hole!

As he creamed my wife's cunt, the coon said,
" I could fuck this until she was dead!"
  As he plugged up her trough,
  I jerked myself off;
" If *that's* how you feel, go ahead!"

1943B.

348

There was a young lady of Spain
Who was fucked by a monk in a drain.
  They did it again,
  And again and again,
And again and again and again.

1943A.

349

Mr. Galsworthy rented a suite
In a building devoid of all heat.
So he fucked for three months,
Sucked thirty-nine cunts,
Which solved his problem quite neat.

1946A.

350

There was a young lady from Sydney
Who could take it right up to her kidney.
But a man from Quebec
Shoved it up to her neck.
He had a long one, now didn' he?

1943B-1952.

351

There was a young man of Tibet,
And this is the strangest one yet—
His prick was so long,
And so pointed and strong,
He could bugger six Greeks *en brochette.*

1941.

352

'Tis said that the Emperor Titius
Had a penchant for pleasantries vicious.
He took two of his nieces
And fucked them to pieces,
And said it was simply delicious.

1941.

353

There was a young man from Toledo
Who was cursed with excessive libido.
To fuck and to screw,
And to fornicate too,
Were the three major points of his credo.

1939A.

354

A virile young man of Touraine
Had vesicles no one could drain.
With an unbroken flow
Thrice the course he would go,
Then roll over and start in again.

1943A.

355

" Far dearer to me than my treasure, "
The heiress declared, " is my leisure.
For then I can screw
The whole Harvard crew—
They're slow, but that lengthens the pleasure. "

1941.

356

A certain old harpy from Umsk
Who was wholly unable to cumsk
Would ecstatically shout
When a samovar spout
Was shoved up her Muscovite rumpsk.

1945.

357

A young man with a passion quite vast
Used to talk about making it last,
Till one day he discovered
His sister uncovered,
And now he fucks often—and fast.

1948A.

358

A galactic patrolman from Venus
Had a hyper-extensible penis.
Of all forms of life
Which he'd taken to wife
He preferred a mere woman, from meanness.

1944.

359

The sex of the asteroid vermin
Is exceedingly hard to determine.
The galactic patrol
Simply fucks any hole
That will possibly let all the sperm in.

1944.

360

There was a young fellow from Wark
Who, when he screws, has to bark.
His wife is a bitch
With a terrible itch,
So the town never sleeps after dark.

1946A.

361

There was a debauched little wench
Whom nothing could ever make blench.
She admitted men's poles
At all possible holes,
And she'd bugger, fuck, jerk off, and french.

1943.

362

There's an over-sexed lady named Whyte
Who insists on a dozen a night.
A fellow named Cheddar
Had the brashness to wed her—
His chance of survival is slight.

1941.

363

There was a Hell's Kitchen Y.T.
Who said to two boyfriends, " Aw, gee,
I don't think that coitus
Could possibly hoit us! "
So they did it together, all three.

1943B-1944A.

364

A versatile lady of Zaandam
Made appointments completely at random,
    Since if two dates got mixed
    It was easily fixed
By letting them screw her in tandem.

1949.

365

While fucking one night, Dr. Zuck
His wife's nipples in his ears stuck.
    Then, his thumb up her bum,
    He could hear himself come,
Thus inventing the Radio Fuck.

Then on further experiment bent,
An improvement he thought he'd invent:
    With his prick as conductor,
    Combed her bush while he fucked her,
And his balls shot off sparks when she spent.

1941.

367

Here's to it, and through it, and to it again,
To suck it, and screw it, and screw it again!
    So in with it, out with it,
    Lord work his will with it!
Never a day we don't do it again!

1880-1941*

368

It's only human nature after all
If a fellow puts a girl against the wall
    And puts his inclination
    Into her accomodation
    To increase the population
    Of the rising generation—
Why, it's only human nature after all.

1943-1946A.

369. THEY A' DO'T

The grit folk an' the puir do't,
The blyte folk an' the sour do't,
    The black, the white,
    Rude an' polite,
Baith autocrat an' boor do't.

For they a' do't—they a' do't,
The beggars an' the braw do't,
    Folk that ance were,
    An' folk that are—
The folk that come will a' do't.

    The auld folk try't
    The young ane's spy't,
An' straightway kiss an' fa' to't,*
    The blind, the lame,
    The wild, the tame,
In warm climes an' in cauld do't.

The licensed by the law do't,
Forbidden folk an' a' do't,
    An' priest an' nun
    Enjoy the fun,
An' never ance say na' to't.

The goulocks an' the snails do't,
The cushie-doos an' quails do't,
    The dogs, the cats,
    The mice, the rats,
E'en elephants an' whales do't.

The weebit cocks an' hens do't,
The robins an' the wrens do't,
    The grizzly bears,
    The toads an' hares,
The puddocks in the fens do't.

The boars an' kangaroos do't,
The titlins an' cuckoos do't,
    While sparrows sma'
    An' rabbits a'
In countless swarms an' crews do't.

The midges, fleas, an' bees do't,
The mawkes an' mites in cheese do't,
    An' cauld earthworms
    Crawl up in swarms,
An' underneath the trees do't.

The kings an' queens an' a' do't,
The Sultan an' Pacha do't,
    An' Spanish dons
    Loup off their thrones
Pu' doon their breeks, an' fa' to't.

For they a' do't—they a' do't,
The grit as weel's the sma' do't,
    Frae crowned king
    To creeping thing,
'Tis just the same—they a' do't!

1832*-1880.

IV

ORAL IRREGULARITY

379

There once was a lady from Arden
Who sucked off a man in a garden.
He said, " My dear Flo,
Where does all that stuff go ? "
And she said, " (*swallow hard*)—I beg pardon ? "

1932.

380

Said a man to a maid of Ashanti,
"Can one sniff of your twitchet, or can't he ?"
Said she with a grin,
" Sure, shove your nose in!
But *presto,* please—not too *andante.* "

1941.

381

There was a young fairy named Bates
Who took out young fellows on dates.
With his hands on their hips
He applied his hot lips
To their phalluses, testes, and nates.

1947-1951.

382

There was a young girl in Berlin
Who eked out a living through sin.
She didn't mind fucking,
But much preferred sucking,
And she'd wipe off the pricks on her chin.

1941.

383

A fastidious young fop of Bhogat
Would suck a girl's cunt, just like that,
    But he'd wipe off her jib,
    And then slip on a bib,
To make sure not to soil his cravat.

1941.

384

There was a young lass of Blackheath
Who frigged an old man with her teeth.
    She complained that he stunk
    Not so much from the spunk,
But his arsehole was just underneath.

1870.

385

An explorer whose habits were blunt
Once flavored some cannibal cunt.
    The asshole was shitty,
    And—more was the pity—
It oozed from the rear to the front.

1946A.

386

In his youth our old friend Boccaccio
Was having a girl in a patio.
    When it came to the twat
    She wasn't so hot,
But, boy, was she good at fellatio!

1939A-1948A.

387

There was an old fellow of Brest
Who sucked off his wife with a zest.
    Despite her great howls
    He sucked out her bowels,
And spat them all over her chest.

1927-1928.

388

There was a young fellow of Buckingham,
Wrote a treatise on cunts and on sucking them,
But later this work
Was eclipsed by a Turk
Whose topic was ass-holes and fucking them.

1879-1941.

389

There was a young bride, a Canuck,
Told her husband, " Let's do more than suck.
You say that I, maybe,
Can have my first baby—
Let's give up this Frenching, and fuck! "

1943B-1944A.

390

King Louis gave a lesson in Class,
One time he was sexing a lass.
When she used the word " Damn "
He rebuked her : " Please ma'am,
Keep a more civil tongue in my ass. "

1950.

391

There was an old bugger of Como
Who suddenly cried : " Ecce homo! "
He tracked his man down
To the heart of the town,
And gobbled him off in the duomo.

1928.

392

A fellatrix' healthful condition
Proved the value of spunk as nutrition.
Her remarkable diet
(I suggest that you try it)
Was only her clients' emission.

1952.

393

A pert miss named Mary Contrary
Was attacked by a man on a ferry.
When he'd done he said, " Come
On now, swallow my scum! "
" I won't—but I want to, " said Mary.

1944A.

394

There was a young man named Isaac Cox
Who took as his motto, " I suck cocks. "
This frank declaration
Brought him such reputation
That he spent twenty years sucking cocks on the docks.

1942-1951.

395

A girl with a sebaceous cyst
Always came when her ass-hole was kissed.
Her lover was gratified
That she was so satisfied,
But regretted the fun that he missed.

1948A.

396

The nephew of one of the czars
Used to suck off Rasputin at Yars,
Till the peasants revolted,
The royal family bolted—
Now they're under the sickle and stars.

1952.

397

There once was a cuntlapper's daughter
Who, despite all her father had taught her,
Would become so unstrung
At the touch of a tongue
That she'd deluge her beau with her water.

1941.

398

There was an old man of Decatur,
Took out his red-hot pertater.
He tried at her dent
But when his thing bent,
He got down on his knees and he ate 'er.

1927.

399

There once was a maid in Duluth,
A striver and seeker of truth.
This pretty wench
Was adept at French,
And said all else was uncouth.

1927.

400

A progressive and young Eskimo
Grew tired of his squaw, and so
Slipped out of his hut
To look for a slut
Who knew the very fine art of Blow.

1946A.

401

There was a young lady named Grace
Who took all she could in her face,
But an adequate lad
Gave her all that he had,
And blew tonsils all over the place.

1943A.

402

That naughty old Sappho of Greece
Said, " What I prefer to a piece
Is to have my pudenda
Rubbed hard by the enda
The little pink nose of my niece."

1928-1932.

403

There was a young Jewess named Hannah
Who sucked off her lover's banana.
She swore that the cream
That shot out in a stream
Tasted better than Biblical manna.

1942.

404

There was a young lady named Hix
Who was fond of sucking big pricks.
One fellow she took
Was a doctor named Snook,
Now *he's* in a hell of a fix.

1952*

405

A Roman of old named Horatio
Was fond of a form of fellatio.
He kept accurate track
Of the boys he'd attack,
And called it his cock-sucking ratio.

1943.

406

The priests at the temple of Isis
Used to offer up amber and spices,
Then back of the shrine
They would play 69
And other unmentionable vices.

1942A.

407

There was an old man from Keith
Who never could get any pieth
By asking young men
If they hadn't the yen
To get sucked off by one without teeth.

1942-1952.

408

There was a young bounder named Link
Who possessed a very tart dink.
    To sweeten it some
    He steeped it in rum,
And he's driven the ladies to drink.

1946A.

409

There lived in French Louisiana
A quaint and deceived old duenna
    Who naively thought
    That a penis was wrought
To be et like a thick ripe banana.

1952.

410

There was an old maid from Luck
Who took it into her head to fuck.
    She was about to resign
    Till she hung out a sign:
" Come in, I've decided to suck. "

1943.

411

Aren't you a trifle atavistic, Mac,
With that little supernumerary nipple on your sac?
    When I go down to eat
    My purpose I defeat
When my lips slip from meat to teat and back.

1942.

412

A canny Scotch lass named McFargle,
Without coaxing and such argy-bargle,
    Would suck a man's pud
    Just as hard as she could,
And she saved up the sperm for a gargle.

1941.

413

Said the priest to Miss Bridget McLennin,
" Sure, a kiss of your twat isn't sinnin'."
And he stuck to this story
Till he tasted the gory
And menstruous state she was then in.

1941.

414

A Lesbian lady named Maud
Got into the Wacs by a fraud.
With a tongue long and knobby
She raped Col. Hobby,
And now she's a major, by god!

1944A.

415

There was a young fellow named Meek
Who invented a lingual technique.
It drove women frantic
And made them romantic,
And wore all the hair off his cheek.

1945.

416

" It 's dull in Duluth, Minnesota,
Of spirit there's not an iota— "
Complained Alice to Joe,
Who tried not to show
That he yawned in her snatch as he blowed her.

1952.

417

There was a young man of Nantucket
Whose prick was so long he could suck it.
He said with a grin,
As he wiped off his chin,
" If my ear were a cunt I could fuck it. "

1927-1928.

418

Nantucketensis ridebat
Penem longiorem sugebat:
  Si auris machina
  Aut potens vagina
Libenter ingredi potebat.

1941.

419

A socialite out on Nantucket
Had a twat that was wide as a bucket.
  She proclaimed, " If it's clean
  I will take it between—
If it's rotten I'd far better suck it. "

1942A.

420

There once was an Anglican pastor
Whose maid didn't let much get past her.
  She said, " When you muff-dive on
  The living-room divan.
Please use an anti-macassar. "

1948A.

421

There was a young fellow named Pell
Who didn't like cunt very well.
  He would finger and fuck one,
  But never would suck one—
He just couldn't get used to the smell.

1941.

422

There once was a brilliant young poet
Who loved it—wouldn't you know it?
  When you'd want to six nine
  His penis would pine.
" I just can't, " it said; " I can't go it. "

1942.

423

" At a séance, " said a young man named Post,
" I was being sucked off by a ghost;
 Someone switched on the lights
 And there in gauze tights,
On his knees, was Tobias mine host. "

1948A.

424

There was a young dancer, Priscilla,
Who flavored her cunt with vanilla.
 The taste was so fine,
 Men and beasts stood in line,
Including a stud armadilla.

1943B.

425

An old doctor who lacked protoplasm
Tried to give his young wife an orgasm,
 But his tongue jumped the track
 'Twixt the front and the back.
And got pinched in a bad anal spasm.

1947.

426

There once was a man of Sag Harbor
Who used to go *with* a fag barber.
 He gave some auditions
 In many positions,
And now he plays flute with Jan Garber.

1947B.

427

There was a young man of Saint Kitts
Who was very much troubled with fits.
 After chewing a gal's cunt
 He'd give a loud grunt
And try to bite off her two teats.

1946A.

428

A young bride was once heard to say,
" Oh dear, I am wearing away!
The insides of my thighs
Look just like mince pies,
For my husband won't shave every day. "

1943A.

429

There was a young man of Soho
Whose tastes were exceedingly low.
He said to his mother,
" Let us suck one another,
And swallow the seminal flow. "

1882.

430

An Indian squaw up at Spruce
Was unable to have a papoose.
She said to her pater,
When he asked, " What's the matter? "
" I can't swallow the foul, slimy juice. "

1946A-1952.

431

A worried young man from Stamboul
Discovered red spots on his tool.
Said the doctor, a cynic,
" Get out of my clinic!
Just wipe off the lipstick, you fool. "

1944A-1952.

432

A tidy young lady of Streator
Dearly loved to nibble a peter.
She always would say,
" I prefer it this way.
I think it is very much neater. "

1927-1941.

433

Old Louis Quatorze was hot stuff.
He tired of that game, blindman's buff,
Up-ended his mistress,
Kissed hers while she kissed his,
And thus taught the world *soixante-neuf*.

1943B.

434

There's a dowager near Sweden Landing
Whose manners are odd and demanding.
It's one of her jests
To suck off her guests—
She hates to keep gentlemen standing.

1952.

435

There was a young girl, very sweet,
Who thought sailors' meat quite a treat.
When she sat on their lap
She unbuttoned their flap,
And always had plenty to eat.

1944-1952.

436

There was a young fellow named Taylor
Who seduced a respectable sailor.
When they put him in jail
He worked out the bail
By licking the parts of the jailer.

1941A.

437

There was a young lady, and what do you think?
She said, " I care nought for a prick that don't stink,
And I think that a fuck
Ain't so good as a suck
When you've pulled back the foreskin and uncovered the pink."

1870.

438

Have you heard of young Franchot Tone,
Who felt of his own peculiar bone?
It was long and quite narrow
And filled full of marrow,
And less edible than stale corn pone.

1942.

439

A caddy named Tommy the Tough
Had an heiress way out in the rough.
He said, " What a swell fuck!
Now let's you and me suck—
Or as you uppercrust say, 'Soixante-neuf'. "

1948A.

440

There was an old lady of Troy
Who invented a new kind of joy:
She sugared her quim,
And frosted the rim,
And then had it sucked by a boy.

1879-1941.

441

There was a young lady called Tucker,
And the parson he tried hard to fuck her.
She said, " You gay sinner,
Instead of your dinner,
At my cunt you shall have a good suck, ah."

1870.

442

There was a young fellow named Tucker
Who, instructing a novice cock-sucker,
Said, " Don't bow out your lips
Like an elephant's hips,
The boys like it best when they pucker. "

1934.

443

There was an old Warden of Wadham, he
Was very much given to sodomy,
But he shyly confessed,
" I like tongue-fucking best,
God bless my soul, isn't it odd of me ? "

1870.

444

There was an old party of Wokingham,
And his whores said he always was poking 'em,
But all he could do
Was to tongue-fuck a few,
And sniff at his fingers while roking 'em.

1870.

445

There is a new Baron of Wokingham,
The girls say he don't care for poking 'em,
Preferring " Minette, "
Which is pleasant, but yet,
There is one disadvantage, his choking 'em.

1879.

V

BUGGERY

446

A whimsical Arab from Aden,
His masculine member well laden,
  Cried : " Nuptial joy,
  When shared with a boy,
Is better than melon or maiden! "

1946B.

447

A pederast living in Arles
Used to bugger the bung of a barrel,
  But was heard to lament,
 " In the old days I went
Up the blue-blooded bum of an earl! "

1942A.

448

There was a young man of Arras
Who stretched himself out on the grass,
  And with no little trouble
  He bent himself double
And stuck his prick well up his ass.

1941.

449

A convict once, out in Australia,
Said unto his turnkey, " I'll tail yer. "
  But he said, " You be buggered,
  You filthy old sluggard,
You're forgetting as I am your gaoler. "

1870.

450

There was a young man from Axminster
Whose designs were quite base and quite sinister.
His lifelong ambition
Was anal coition
With the wife of the French foreign minister.

1950.

451

A young man who lived in Balbriggan
Went to sea to recover from frigging,
But after a week
As they climbed the fore-peak
He buggered the mate in the rigging.

1942A.

452

Berries, berries, all kinds of berries,
Chancres on her ass like California cherries.
The first time I hit her
I nearly broke her shitter,
Down where the Hasiampa flows.

1927.

453

There was a young party of Bicester
Who wanted to bugger his sister,
But not liking dirt,
He bought him a squirt,
And cleaned out her arse with a clyster.

1879.

454

Some night when you're drunk on Dutch Bols
Try changing the usual rôles.
The backward position
Is nice for coition
And it offers the choice of two holes.

1947B.

455

There was a young belle from Bombay
Who never had thought herself gay,
    Till a quean from Siam
    Said, " My dear, you're not jam! "
And brought that one out right away.

1942.

456

There was a brave damsel of Brighton
Whom nothing could possibly frighten.
    She plunged in the sea
    And, with infinite glee,
Was fucked in the ass by a Triton.

1952.

457

As he lay in his bath, mused Lord Byng,
" Oh Vimy! What memories you bring!
    That gorgeous young trooper...
    No! No! Gladys Cooper!
By Gad, sir! That was a near thing. "

1945A.

458

Coitus upon a cadaver
Is the ultimate way you can have 'er.
    Her inanimate state
    Means a man needn't wait,
And eliminates all the palaver.

1940*-1947B.

459

There was a young man of Calcutta
    Who thought he would do a smart trick,
So anointed his arsehole with butter,
    And in it inserted his prick.
    It was not for greed after gold,
    It was not for thirst after pelf;
    Twas simply because he'd been told
    To bloody well bugger himself.

1879.

460.

A Phi Delt known as Carruthers
Will never make little girls mothers.
Around the old brown
He is covered with down
To wipe off the dongs of his brothers.

1942.

461.

There was a young man from Chubut
Who had a remarkable root:
When hard it would bend
With a curve at the end,
So he fucked himself in the petoot.

1942.

462

A parson who lived near Cremorne
Looked down on all women with scorn.
E'en a boy's white, fat bum
Could not make him come,
But an old man's piles gave him the horn.

1879.

463

There was a young fellow named Dave
Who kept a dead whore in a cave.
He said, " I admit
I'm a bit of a shit,
But think of the money I save! "

1927-1939A.

464

There was a young Jew of Delray
Who buggered his father one day.
He said, " I like rather
To stuff it up Father;
He's clean, and there's nothing to pay. "

1879-1928.

465

A depraved old Jew from Estretto
Buggered every young man in the ghetto.
He once had his hose in
A musician, composing,
Who said: " Not so slow—allegretto! "

1946B.

466

A mortician who practised in Fife
Made love to the corpse of his wife.
" How could I know, Judge?
She was cold, did not budge—
Just the same as she'd acted in life. "

1942A.

467

A glutted debauchee from Frome
Lured beauteous maids to his room,
Where, after he'd strip 'em,
He'd generally whip 'em
With a bundle of twigs or a broom.

1945.

468

When she wanted a new way to futter
He greased her behind with butter;
Then, with a sock,
In went his jock,
And they carried her home on a shutter.

1927.

469

There was a young pansy named Gene
Who cruised a sadistic Marine.
Said the man with a smirk
As they got down to work,
" In this game the Jack beats the Queen. "

1943A.

470

There was a young lady of Glasgow,
And fondly her lover did ask, "Oh,
Pray allow me a fuck,"
But she said, "No, my duck,
But you may, if you please, up my arse go."

1879.

471

At the *Iphigenia* of Gluck
Two ushers attempted to fuck.
At the blare of the brass
One contracted his ass,
And they carted him off in a truck.

1947B.

472

There was an old man named Grasty
Whose favorite sport was ass-ty.
He'd bugger with joy
Any innocent boy,
But thought fornication was nasty.

1927.

473

A native of Havre de Grace
Once tired of Cunt, said, "I'll try arse."
He unfolded his plan
To another young man,
Who said, "Most decidedly, my arse!"

1879.

474

There was a young fellow named Howell
Who buggered himself with a trowel.
The triangular shape
Was conducive to rape,
And was easily cleaned with a towel.

1941A.

475

A prisoner in Château d'If
Ran around on all fours for a sniff
Of his comrade's posterior,
And said, " It's inferior,
But it somehow reminds me of quiff. "

1942A.

476

A Sultan of old Istamboul
Had a varicose vein in his tool.
This evoked joyous grunts
From his harem of cunts,
But his boys suffered pain at the stool.

1928-1949.

477

Said an airy young fairy named Jess,
" The oral requires some finesse,
While in method the anal
Is terribly banal,
And the trousers will get out of press. "

1943A.

478

A psychiatrist fellow, quite Jung,
Asked his wife, " May I bugger your bung? "
And was so much annoyed
When he found her a-Freud,
He went out in the yard and ate dung.

1941.

479

There was a young reb from Kadoches
Who had a hospitable toches.
His friends had no fear
To attack from the rear,
For he'd make it quite kosher with broches.

1943C.

480

An embalmer in ancient Karnak
Oozed it into a fresh corpse's crack.
    Rigor mortis set in
    And clamped off what had been
His pride, nor did he get it back.

1942A.

481

There was a young fellow named Kelly
Who preferred his wife's ass to her belly.
    He shrieked with delight
    As he ploughed through the shite,
And filled up her hole with his jelly.

1942.

482

There was an old man of Kentucky,
Said to his old woman, " Oi'll fuck ye. "
    She replied, " Now you wunt
    Come anigh my old cunt,
For your prick is all stinking and mucky. "

1870.

483

There was an old phoney named Kinsey
Whose ideas of fucking were flimsy.
    He knew how to measure
    A penis for pleasure,
But he came much too quick in a quim, see?

1952.

484

There was a young man from Liberia
Who was forced to flee to the interior.
    He'd buggered a brother,
    His father and mother—
He considered his sisters inferior.

1947B-1952.

485

A youth who seduced a poor lighterman,
Said, " I'd much sooner fuck than I'd fight a man,
    And although, Sir, I find
    You a very good grind,
I must say I've had a much tighter man. "

1870.

486

A young nigger boxer, Joe Louis,
Who buggered a bastardly Jewess,
    He said with a sigh
    As his engine went dry,
" I wonder where all of my goo is. "

1939A.

487

There was a young mate of a lugger
Who took out a girl just to hug her.
  " I've my monthlies, " she said,
  " And a cold in the head,
But my bowels work well... Do you bugger? "

1928.

488

There was a young man of Madras
Who was having a boy in the grass.
    Then a cobra-capello
    Said, " Hello, young fellow! "
And bit a piece out of his arse.

1928.

489

There was a young priest from Madrid
Who looked with lewd eyes on a kid.
    He said, " With great joy
    I could bugger that boy.
I'll be damned if I don't! "— And he did.

1927A-1939A.

490

There was a hermaphrodite kid,
Made a pass at a man from Madrid.
" Why, you son of a maggot,
Do you think *I'm* a faggot?
Just go fuck yourself! "— So he did.

1943B.

491

There was a young lady whose mind
Was never especially refined.
She got on her knees,
Her lover to please,
Who stuck in his prick from behind.

1939*

492

There once was a well-groomed young nance
Who responded to every advance,
But rather than strip
He let anything slip
Through a hole in the seat of his pants.

1942.

493

There was a young man from Nantasket
Who screwed a dead whore in a casket.
He allowed 'twas no vice,
But thought it was nice,
For she needed no money, nor'd ask it.

1947B.

494

There was a young man from Nantucket
Who had such a big cock he could suck it.
He looked in the glass
And saw his own ass,
And broke his neck trying to fuck it.

1939A-1946A.

495

Should a fellow discover some night
A girl's body in bed, it's all right.
He should think it good luck,
And accept the free fuck—
He will bugger her too, if he's bright.

1941.

496

There was a Captain of MAG 94
More easily had than a two-bit whore.
He wanted to drink
And fondle your dink,
But he's not around any more.

1945C.

497

There once was a doughty Norwegian
Who enlivened the French Foreign Legion,
But his brothers-in-arms
Who succumbed to his charms
All got clap in their hindermost region.

1941.

498

There was a young fellow named Oakum
Whose brags about fucking were hokum,
For he really preferred
To suck cocks and stir turd—
He was Queen of the Flits in Hoboken.

1941.

499

Said Oscar McDingle O'Figgle,
With an almost hysterical giggle,
"Last night I was sick
With delight when my prick
Felt dear Alfred's delicious arse wriggle!"

1941.

500

There was a young man of Oswego,
Whose friends said, "Be off now, to sea go."
He there learned the trick
Of skinning his prick,
And up arses thrusting his pego.

1870.

501

A young queer who was much oversexed
Was easily fretted and vexed.
When out on a date
He hardly could wait
To say, "Turn over, bud; my turn next."

1942-1952.

502

There was a young man of Peru
Who dreamt he was had by a Jew.
He woke up at night
In a hell of a fright,
And found it was perfectly true.

1928.

503

There were three young men in Peru:
A German, a bugger, a Jew.
The German he buggered
The bugger, the bugger!
The bugger, he buggered the Jew.

1941.

504

There was an old man from Pinole
Who always got in the wrong hole,
And when he withdrew,
All covered with goo,
His temper was out of control.

1942.

505

A phenomenal fellow named Preston
Has a hair-padded lower intestine.
Though exceedingly fine
In the buggery line,
It isn't much good for digestin'.

1952.

506

A man who is lacking in pride
Attends funerals far, near, and wide.
When asked about this
His reply is, "It's bliss
To bugger a piece of dead hide."

1946A.

507

"I'll do it for Art—I'm no prude!"
He said, as he posed in the nude.
But on viewing his ass
The whole fairy class
Decided it ought to be screwed.

1946A-1952.

508

There was an old man of Ramnugger
Who drove a rare trade as a bugger,
Till a fair young Circassian
Brought fucking in fashion,
And spoilt all the trade in Ramnugger.

1870.

509

There once was an apple-cheeked runt
Who was welcomed with joy at the Front.
This God's gift to he-men
Prevented spilled semen,
For his ass was tattooed like a cunt.

1947B.

510. ROYAL SPASM IN FIVE FITS

Thus spake the King of Siam :
" For women I don't care a damn.
  But a fat-bottomed boy
  Is my pride and my joy—
They call me a bugger : I am. "

" Indeed, " quoth the King of Siam,
" For cunts I just don't give a damn.
  They haven't the grip,
  Nor the velvety tip,
Nor the scope of the ass-hole of man. "

Then up spake the Bey of Algiers
And said to his harem, " My dears,
  You may think it odd o' me
  But I've given up sodomy—
Tonight there'll be fucking! " (*Loud cheers.*)

Then up spake the young King of Spain :
" To fuck and to bugger is pain.
  But it's not *infra dig*
  On occasion to frig,
And I do it again and again. "

Then up spoke a Hindu mahout,
And said, " What's all this blithering about?
  Why, I shoot my spunk
  Up an elephant's trunk— "
(*Cries of* " Shame! He's a shit! Throw him out! ")

1910-1938*

515

There was a young lady named Spruce
Whose favorite thrill was a goose.
Just the sight of a thumb
Made her tokus all numb,
And her bowels got excited—and loose.

1941.

516

In Glasgow a tender tapeworm
Was so starved that he barely could squirm,
Until his host finally
Was buggered divinely,
And Jimmie had vaseline and sperm.

1942A.

517

Meet Elmer, young son of the Thorpes,
Afflicted with psychotic warps.
His idea of fun
Is to bugger a nun,
And then vomit all over the corpse.

1946A.

518

An earnest young woman in Thrace
Said, "Darling, that's not the right place!"
So he gave her a thwack,
And did on her back
What he couldn't have done face to face.

1942A.

519

Close to 'long ass b'long coconut tree,
One fellow mary come up 'long me,
Si' down long grass,
Igot big fellow ass,
Italk ilike push-push 'long me.

1946.

520

There was a young colonel from Trent
Who lived in a lavender tent.
He said that some sessions
With interesting Hessians
Had taught him what war really meant.

1942.

521. WHO'LL BUGGER THE TURK?

" I, " said Gladstone, " as Chief of the Nation,
And Premier of England, to gain reputation.
I'll bugger the Turk,
And ne'er let him shirk
My prick's Grand Demonstration! "

1880.

522

Said Senator David I. Walsh,
" These charges against me are falsh.
Though I did go to Brooklyn
For sooklyn and fooklyn,
Not a gob laid his hands on my balsh. "

1947B.

523. THE GOOD SHIP VENUS

The good ship's name was Venus,
Her mast a towering penis,
Her figure-head
A whore in bed—
A pretty sight, by Jesus!

The first mate's name was Andy,
By God, he was a dandy,
They broke his cock
With chunks of rock
For conking in the brandy.

The second mate was Morgan,
By God, he was a Gorgon,
Nine times a day
Fine tunes he'd play
On his reproductive organ.

The captain's daughter Mabel
They screwed when they were able,
They nailed her tits,
Those lousy shits,
Right to the captain's table.

The captain's other daughter,
They threw her in the water,
You could tell by the squeals
That some of the eels
Had found her reproductive quarter.

The cabin-boy*
Was the captain's joy,
A cunning little nipper,
They filled his ass
With broken glass
And circumcized the skipper.

Then in search of new sensation
In the forms of recreation,
The ship was sunk
In a wave of gunk
From mutual masturbation.

1946A.

VI

ABUSES OF THE CLERGY

530

There was a young lady named Alice
Who peed in a Catholic chalice.
  She said, " I do this
  From a great need to piss,
And not from sectarian malice. "

1941.

531

There was a young girl in Alsace
Who was having her first piece of ass.
 " Oh, darling, you'll kill me!
  Oh, dearest, you thrill me
Like Father John's thumb after mass! "

1947.

532

A modern monk nicknamed Augustin,
His penis a boy's bottom thrust in.
  Then said Father Ignatius,
 " Now really! Good gracious!
Your conduct is really disgusting. "

1870.

533

There was a young pansy named Birch
Who developed a taste for the church,
  And monks, priests, and preachers,
  And such mouthy creatures,
Were the uplifted ends of his search.

1941.

534

There were three young ladies of Birmingham,
And this is the scandal concerning 'em.
They lifted the frock
And tickled the cock
Of the Bishop engaged in confirming 'em.

Now, the Bishop was nobody's fool,
He'd been to a good public school,
So he took down their britches
And buggered those bitches
With his ten-inch episcopal tool.

Then up spoke a lady from Kew,
And said, as the Bishop withdrew,
"The vicar is quicker
And thicker and slicker,
And longer and stronger than you."

1927A-1941*

537

There was a young Bishop from Brest
Who openly practiced incest.
"My sisters and nieces
Are all dandy pieces,
And they don't cost a cent," he confessed.

1945.

538

There was a young curate of Buckingham
Who was blamed by the girls for not fucking 'em.
He said, "Though my cock
Is as hard as a rock,
Your cunts are too slack. Put a tuck in 'em."

1928.

539

There was a young lady of Cheyne
Who crept into the vestry unseen.
She pulled down her knickers,
And also the vicar's,
And said, " How about it, old bean? "

1941.

540

There was a young lady of Chichester
Who made all the saints in their niches stir.
One morning at matins
Her breasts in white satins
Made the Bishop of Chichester's britches stir.

1939A-1941.

541

A young curate, just new to the cloth,
At sex was surely no sloth.
He preached masturbation
To his whole congregation,
And was washed down the aisle on the froth.

1946B.

542

I once had the wife of a Dean
Seven times while the Dean was out ski'in'.
She remarked with some gaiety,
" Not bad for the laity,
Though the Bishop once managed thirteen. "

1947B.

543

There was a young choir-boy from Devon
Who was raped in a hay-stack by seven
High Anglican priests—
(Lascivious beasts)—
For of such is the kingdom of heaven.

1941-1943A.

544

There was a young monk from Dundee
Who hung a nun's cunt on a tree.
He grabbed her fair ass
And performed a high mass
That even the Pope came to see.

1947A.

545

There was a young curate of Eltham
Who wouldn't fuck girls, but he felt 'em.
In lanes he would linger
And play at stink-finger,
And *scream* with delight when he smelt 'em.

1879-1935*

546

A Big Catholic Layman named Fox
Makes his living by sucking off cocks.
In spells of depression
He goes to confession,
And jacks off the priest in his box.

The priest, a cocksucker named Sheen,
Is delighted their sins aren't seen.
"Though God sees through walls,"
Says Monsignor, "— Oh, balls!
This God stuff is simply a screen."

1945-1951.

548

There was an archbishop in France
Who saw a nude woman by chance.
The result, I affirm,
Was emission of sperm
In the archiepiscopal pants.

1941.

549

There once was a priest of Gibraltar
Who wrote dirty jokes in his psalter.
  An inhibited nun
  Who had read every one
Made a vow to be laid on his altar.

1938.

550

There was a young lady named Jessary
Got deflowered while in a confessary.
  The priest who thus wrecked her
  Would scorn a protector,
While she'd never heard of a pessary!

1943B.

551

There was an old Abbot of Khief
Who thought the Impenitent Thief
  Had bollocks of brass
  And an amethyst arse.
He died in this awful belief.

1928.

552

There was a young monk of Kilkyre,
Was smitten with carnal desire.
  The immediate cause
  Was the abbess' drawers,
Which were hung up to dry by the fire.

1941.

553

There was a young rector of Kings
Whose mind was on heavenly things,
  But his heart was on fire
  For a boy in the choir
Whose ass was like jelly on springs.

1941.

554

Apud Rege tutor veteramus
Puellaria odit profanus
Semper optandus
Pueri sperandus
Gellifactus in siliis anus.

1941.

555

When a lecherous curate at Leeds
Was discovered, one day, in the weeds
Astride a young nun,
He said, "Christ, this is fun!
Far better than telling one's beads!"

1946B.

556

A Sunday-School student in Mass.
Soon rose to the head of the class,
By reciting quite bright
And by sleeping at night
With his tongue up the minister's ass.

1941.

557

In Kansas there lived a young monk
Who often was in a blue funk,
For his come always froze
On the sisters' thick hose,
And they never would part with a chunk.

1952.

558

A lecherous Bishop of Peoria,
In a state of constant euphoria,
Enjoyed having fun
With a whore or a nun
While chanting the Sanctus and Gloria.

1944-1945.

559

There was a gay rector of Poole
Most deservedly proud of his tool.
With some trifling aid
From the curate, 'tis said,
He rogered the National School.

1870.

560

A hoary old monk of Regina
Once said, "There is nothing diviner
Than to sit in one's cell
And let one's mind dwell
On the charms of the Virgin's vagina."

1941-1947B.

561

There was a young man of St. Giles
Who'd walked thousands and thousands of miles,
From the Cape of Good Hope,
Just to bugger the Pope,
But he couldn't — the pontiff had piles.

1941.

562

There was an old abbess quite shocked
To find nuns where the candles were locked.
Said the abbess, "You nuns
Should behave more like guns,
And never go off till you're cocked."

1941.

563

There was a young monk of Siberia
Who of frigging grew weary and wearier.
At last, with a yell,
He burst from his cell,
And buggered the Father Superior.

1879-1928.

564

There was a young monk from Siberia
Whose morals were very inferior.
He did to a nun
What he shouldn't have done,
And now she's a Mother Superior.

1933*-1941.

565

Three lustful young ladies of Simms
Were blessed with such over-size quims,
The bishop of their diocese
Got elephantiasis,
For his life wasn't all singing hymns.

1941.

566

A mediaeval recluse named Sissions
Was alarmed by his nightly emissions.
His cell-mate, a sod,
Said, " Leave it to God. "
And taught him some nifty positions.

1941.

567

There once was a Bishop of Treet
Who decided to be indiscreet,
But after one round
To his horror he found
You repeat, and repeat, and repeat.

1944.

568

A Bishop whose See was Vermont
Used to jerk himself off in the font.
The baptistry stank
With an odor most rank,
And no one would sit up in front.

1952.

569

Said a Palestine pilgrim named Wadham,
" For religion I don't give a goddem!
    I've frequently peed in
    The Garden of Eden,
And buggered my guide when in Sodom. "

1952.

570

The bishop of Winchester Junction
Found his phallus would no longer function.
    So in black crêpe he wound it,
    Tied a lily around it,
And solemnly gave it last unction.

1941.

571

A handsome young monk in a wood
Told a girl she should cling to the good.
    She obeyed him, and gladly;
    He repulsed her, but sadly:
" My dear, you have misunderstood. "

1943A.

572

    The Dean undressed
    With heaving breast,
The bishop's wife to lie on.
    He thought it lewd
    To do it nude,
So he kept his old school tie on.

1941-1942.

573

The Book of God's beneath you,
The Man of God's above you.
    Salvation pole
    Is in your hole—
Now wiggle your ass to save your soul.

1928A-1939*

VII

ZOOPHILY

574

There was a young man of Adair
Who thought he would diddle a mare.
  He climbed up a ladder
  And jolly well had her,
With his backside a-wave in the air.

1941.

575

There was a young man of Australia
Who went on a wild bacchanalia.
  He buggered a frog,
  Two mice and a dog,
And a bishop in fullest regalia.

1941.

576

There once was a sacred baboon
That lived by the river Rangoon,
  And all of the women
  That came to go swimmin'
He'd bang by the light of the moon.

1941.

577

There was a young man from Bangore
Who was tired and said to his whore,
" If you'll only roll over
  I'll get my dog Rover,
And you can have six inches more."

1939A.

578

There once was a man of Belfast
Whose balls out of iron were cast.
He'd managed somehow
To bugger a sow,
Thus you get pig-iron, at last.

1947B.

579

There was a young man of Bengal
Who went to a fancy dress ball.
Just for a stunt
He dressed up as a cunt
And was fucked by a dog in the hall.

1928-1932.

580

A habit obscene and bizarre
Has taken a-hold of papa:
He brings home young camels
And other odd mammals,
And gives them a go at mama.

1946*-1947.

581

The Communist Party's Earl Browder
Was fucking a girl in a howda.
The elephant's trunk
Somehow got in her cunt
Which, they felt, made it terribly crowded.

1948A.

582

There was a young gaucho named Bruno
Who said, "Screwing is one thing I *do* know.
A woman is fine,
And a sheep is divine,
But a llama is Numero Uno."

1942A-1944A.

583

Said an old taxidermist in Burrell,
As he skilfully mounted a squirrel,
" This excess of tail is
Obstructive to phallus;
One's much better off with a girl."

1942A.

584

There was an old man of the Cape
Who buggered a Barbary ape.
The ape said, " You fool!
You've got a square tool;
You've buggered my arse out of shape."

1879-1928.

585

A fisherman off of Cape Cod
Said, " I'll bugger that tuna, by God! "
But the high-minded fish
Resented his wish,
And nimbly swam off with his rod.

1942A.

586

There once was a man of Cape Nod
Who attempted to bugger a cod,
When up came some scallops
And nibbled his bollops,
And now he's a eunuch, by God.

1930*-1951.

587

Minnehaha was washing her clothes,
Unexpectant of sorrows or woes.
A snake, a side-winder,
Crawled in her behinder,
Wiggled 'round and came out of her nose.

1946A.

588

A sailor indulged in coitus
With a cow of the genus of Cetus.
    Piscatologists thundered,
    Biologists wondered,
At the anchor tattooed on the fœtus.

1942A.

589

A man who was richer than Croesus
Enjoyed being sucked off by feices,
    Till a vicious old hound
    Thought his stake was ground round,
And chewed it completely to pieces.

1942.

590

There once was a fairy named Cyril
Who was had in a wood by a squirrel,
    And he liked it so good
    That he stayed in the wood
Just as long as the squirrel was virile.

1941.

591

There once was a clergyman's daughter
Who detested the pony he bought her
    Till she found that its dong
    Was as hard and as long
As the prayers her father had taught her.

She married a fellow named Tony
Who soon found her fucking the pony.
    Said he, " What's it got,
    My dear, that I've not? "
Sighed she, " Just a yard-long bologna. "

1941.

593

That Harvard don down at El Djim—
Oh, wasn't it nasty of him,
    With the whole hareem randy,
    The sheik himself handy,
To muss up a young camel's quim?

1942A.

594

The eminent Mrs. DeVue
Was born in a cage at the zoo,
    And the curious rape
    Which made her an ape
Is highly fantastic, if true.

945A.

595

There was a young girl of Dundee
Who was raped by an ape in a tree.
    The result was most horrid—
    All ass and no forehead,
Three balls and a purple goatee.

1938.

596

Pine insulensis inevit
Rectum simioli quem scivit
    Proles infrontata
    Horrida glandata
Et semper violare cupivit.

1941.

597

The prior of Dunstan St. Just,
Consumed with erotical lust,
    Raped the bishop's prize fowls,
    Buggered four startled owls
And a little green lizard, that bust.

1948A.

598

There was a young girl of Eau Claire
Who once was attacked by a bear.
While chased in a field
She tripped and revealed
Some meat to the bear that was rare.

1944A.

599

There was a young man of Eau Claire
Who had an affair with a bear,
But the surly old brute
With a snap of her snoot
Left him only one ball and some hair.

1927-1947B.

600

When Theocritus guarded his flock
He piped in the shade of a rock.
It is said that his Muse
Was one of the ewes
With a bum like a pink hollyhock.

1942A.

601

There was a young lady named Florence
Who for fucking professed an abhorrence,
But they found her in bed
With her cunt flaming red,
And her poodle-dog spending in torrents.

1941.

602

There once was a fellow named Fogg
Who attempted to bugger a hog.
While engaged in his frolics
The hog ate his bollix,
And now he's a eunuch, by God.

1930*-1946A.

603

One morning Mahatma Gandhi
Had a hard-on, and it was a dandy.
So he said to his aide,
" Please bring me a maid,
Or a goat, or whatever is handy. "

1941.

604

There once was a man of Geneva
Who buggered a black bitch retriever.
The result was a sow,
Two horses, a cow,
Three lambs and a London coal-heaver.

1930*-1952.

605

There was a young peasant named Gorse
Who fell madly in love with his horse.
Said his wife, " You rapscallion,
That horse is a stallion—
This constitutes grounds for divorce. "

1941-1951.

606

There was an old man from near here,
Got awfully drunk upon beer.
He fell in a ditch
And a son of a bitch
Of a bull dog fucked him in the ear.

1928B.

607

The Mahatma on Mt. Himavat
Opined as he diddled a cat:
" She's a far better piece
Than the Viceroy's niece,
Who has also more fur on her prat. "

1942A.

608

A fox-hound retired from the hunt
For he found that his lobes had grown blunt
To the scent of the fox,
But he still would sniff rocks
For the mystical fragrance of cunt.

1942A.

609

There was a young man with the itch
Who, because he was not at all rich,
Had to harbor his tail
In any female—
A duck or a sow or a bitch.

1941.

610

There was a young fellow named Jim
Whose wife kept a worm in her quim.
It was silly and smelly,
And tickled her belly,
And what the hell was it to *him*?

1944A.

611

A spinster in Kalamazoo
Once strolled after dark by the zoo.
She was seized by the nape,
And raped by an ape,
And she murmured, "A wonderful screw."

And she added, "You're rough, yes, and hairy,
But I hope—yes I do—that I marry
A man with a prick
Half as stiff and as thick
As the kind that you zoo-keepers carry."

1941.

613

All the lady-apes ran from King Kong
For his dong was unspeakably long.
  But a friendly giraffe
  Quaffed his yard and a half,
And ecstatically burst into song.

1941.

614

Said a lovely young lady named Lake,
Pervertedly fond of a snake,
  "If my good friend, the boa,
  Shoots spermatozoa,
What offspring we'll leave in our wake!"

Another young lady would make
Advances to snake after snake.
  Though men she had met
  Got her diaphragm wet,
She wanted her glottis to shake.

1928-1941.

616

In a meadow a man named Llewellyn
Had a dream he was bundling with Helen.
  When he woke he discovered
  A bull had him covered
With ballocks as big as a melon.

1942A.

617

There was an old Scot named McTavish
Who attempted an anthropoid ravish.
  The object of rape
  Was the wrong sex of ape,
And the anthropoid ravished McTavish.

1948A.

618

There was a young man, a Maltese,
Who could even screw horses with ease.
He'd flout natural laws
In this manner because
Of his dong, which hung down to his knees.

1943A.

619

Thus spake an old Chinese mandarin,
"There's a subject I'd like to use candor in:
The geese of Pekin
Are so steepèd in sin
They'd as soon let a man as a gander in."

1941.

620

Here's to old King Montezuma,
For fun he would bugger a puma.
The puma in play
Clawed both balls away—
How's that for animal humor?

1948-1950.

621

There was a young lady of Mott
Who inserted a fly up her twat
And pretended the buzz
Was not what it was
But something she knew it was not.

1943-1949.

622

There was a young lady named Myrtle
Who had an affair with a turtle.
She had crabs, so they say,
In a year and a day,
Which proves that the turtle was fertile.

1927-1941.

623

There was a young man from Nantucket
Took a pig in a thicket to fuck it.
Said the pig, "Oh, I'm queer,
Get away from my rear...
Come around to the front and I'll suck it."

1941.

624

There once was a laddie of Neep
Who demanded everything cheap.
When he wanted to screw
There was nothing to do
But take out his passion on sheep.

1951.

625

There was a young man from New Haven
Who had an affair with a raven.
He said with a grin
As he wiped off his chin,
"Nevermore!"

1943C.

626

There was a young man of Newminster Court
Bugger'd a pig, but his prick was too short.
Said the hog, "It's not nice,
But pray take my advice:
Make tracks, or by the police you'll be caught.

1879.

627

An elderly pervert in Nice
Who was long past desire for a piece
Would jack-off his hogs,
His cows and his dogs,
But his parrot called in the police.

1942A.

628

There was a young man named O'Rourke,
Heard babies were brought by the stork,
So he went to the zoo
And attempted to screw
One old bird—end-result: didn't work.

1951.

629

The notorious Duchess of Peels
Saw a fisherman fishing for eels.
Said she, "Would you mind?—
Shove one up my behind.
I am anxious to know how it feels."

1944A.

630

There was a young man in Peru
Who had nothing whatever to do,
So he flew to the garret
And buggered the parrot,
And sent the result to the zoo.

1879-1941.

631

A gruff anthropoid of Piltdown
Had a strange way of going to town:
With maniacal howls
He would bugger young owls,
And polish his balls on their down.

1942.

632

There was a young Nubian prince
Whose cock would make elephants wince.
Once, while socking the sperm
To a large pachyderm,
He slipped, and he's not been seen since.

1943A.

633

There was an old hostler named Rains,
Possessed of more ballocks than brains.
He stood on a stool
To bugger a mule,
And got kicked in the balls for his pains.

1941.

634

There once was a girl named Miss Randall
Who kept a young bear cub to dandle.
She said, " In a pinch
This bear cub's six-inch
Is almost as good as a candle. "

1944.

635

There was a young lady of Rhodes
Who sinned in unusual modes.
At the height of her fame
She abruptly became
The mother of four dozen toads.

1943A.

636

A nigger in fair St. Domingo
Being blasé and worn, said, " By Jingo,
Blast all women and boys,
I'll try some new joys. "
So he went out and fucked a Flamingo.

1880.

637

There was a young man of St. John's
Who wanted to bugger the swans.
But the loyal hall-porter
Said, " Pray take my daughter!
Them birds are reserved for the dons. "

1928-1941.

638

There was a young man of St. Paul
Whose prick was exceedingly small.
He could bugger a bug
At the edge of a rug,
And the bug hardly felt it at all.

1927-1941.

639

A hermit who lived on St. Roque
Had a lily perfected to poke.
He diddled the donkeys
And meddled with monkeys,
And would have done worse, but it broke.

1942A.

640

There was an old man of Santander
Who attempted to bugger a gander.
But that virtuous bird
Plugged its ass with a turd,
And refused to such low tastes to pander.

There was a young man from Toulouse
Who thought he would diddle a goose.
He hunted and bunted
To get the thing cunted,
But decided it wasn't no use.

1879-1941.

642

There was an old person of Sark
Who buggered a pig in the dark.
The swine, in surprise,
Murmured, "God blast your eyes,
Do you take me for Boulton or Park?"

1879.

643

There once was a sergeant named Schmitt
Who wanted a crime to commit.
He thought raping women
Was a little too common,
So he buggered an aged tomtit.

1944.

644

There was a young lady named Schneider
Who often kept trysts with a spider.
She found a strange bliss
In the hiss of her piss,
As it strained through the cobwebs inside her.

1941.

645

When Brother John wanted a screw
He would stuff a fat cat in a shoe,
Pull up his cassock
And kneel on a hassock,
Trying his damnedest to mew.

1942A.

646

There was a young man of Seattle
Who bested a bull in a battle.
With fire and gumption
He assumed the bull's function,
And deflowered a whole herd of cattle.

1945.

647

There was a young girl from Seattle
Whose hobby was sucking off cattle.
But a bull from the South
Left a wad in her mouth
That made both her ovaries rattle.

1941*-1946B.

648

If Gracie Allen were the last of her sex,
And I were the last of mine,
I'd ease my tool
By fucking a mule
Or even a porcupine.

1939A.

649

A rooster residing in Spain
Used to diddle his hens in the rain.
"I give them a bloody
Good time when it's muddy:
Which keeps them from getting too vain."

1942A.

650

There once was a Dutchman named Spiegle
Who slept with an elegant beagle.
As they crawled into bed
He wistfully said,
"It'll be much better if you wiggle."

1942.

651

Said the famous composer, R. Strauss
When asked why he buggered a mouse:
"Though its cunt is quite tiny
On occasion its heiny
Will stretch quite as big as a house."

1948A.

652

There was a young lady named Sutton
Who said, as she carved up the mutton,
"My father preferred
The last sheep in the herd—
This is one of his children I'm cuttin'."

1948A.

653

When Jupiter hid in a swan
And laid Leda low on the lawn,
  Pled she, " Stick your neck in,
  But please do not peck in
My box, for the lining is gone. "

1942A.

654

There was a young lady from Teal
Who was raped in the lake by an eel.
  One morning at dawn
  She gave birth to a prawn,
Two crabs, and a small baby seal.

1939A-1941.

655

As the rabbi was cutting the throat
Of the annual tribal scape-goat,
  Said the beast, " I will cite you
  As a sodomite! You
Forget what we did on the boat. "

1942A.

656

A novelist from Tortilla Flats
Repeatedly buggered stray cats.
  The alley-fence howls
  As he stirred up their bowels
Enormously pleased the town rats.

1940*

657

A broken-down harlot named Tupps
Was heard to confess in her cups:
  " The height of my folly
  Was fucking a collie—
But I got a nice price for the pups. "

1941.

658

A vice both obscene and unsavory
Holds the Mayor of Southampton in slavery.
With bloodcurdling howls
He deflowers young owls
Which he keeps in an underground aviary.

1939*

659

A sheep-herder out in Van Buren
Lost half of his flock with the murrain.
Quoth the state veterinary,
"You ought not to carry
Them live spirochetes of your'n!"

1942A.

660

There was a young artist named Victor
Who purchased a boa constrictor.
He intended to sketch her,
But decided (the lecher!)
To fuck her instead of depict her.

1943A.

661

A promiscuous person named Willie
Had a dong that was simply a dilly.
He would take on all mammals
And was partial to camels,
But they never could tolerate Willie.

1942-1952.

662

There was a young lady of Wohl's Hill
Who sat herself down on a mole's hill.
The resident mole
Stuck his head up her hole—
The lady's all right, but the mole's ill.

1951.

663

There was a young man in Woods Hole
Who had an affair with a mole.
    Though a bit of a nancy
    He *did* like to fancy
Himself in a dominant role.

1951.

664

You've heard of the Duchess of York,
She's twice been blessed by the stork.
    The Duke will fuck
    Naught else but a duck,
While the Duchess she frequents the park.

1939A.

665

A keeper in Hamburg's great zoo
Tried to have a young girl kangaroo.
    But she zipped up her pouch,
    And the rascal said, " Ouch!
You've got a half peter in you. "

1942A.

VIII

EXCREMENT

666

The Rajah of Afghanistan
Imported a Birmingham can,
Which he set as a throne
On a great Buddha stone—
But he crapped out-of-doors like a man.

1942A.

667

There was a young lady named Ames
Who would play at the jolliest games.
She was great fun to lay
For her rectum would play
Obbligatos, and call you bad names.

1941.

668

A young lady who lived in Astoria
Took a fancy to Fletcher's Castoria.
She partook of this drink
With her ass in the sink—
Now I ask you : ain't that foresight for ya ?

1948A.

669

When a woman in strapless attire
Found her breasts working higher and higher,
A guest, with great feeling,
Exclaimed, "How appealing!
Do you mind if I piss in the fire ?"

1945.

670

Sir Reginald Barrington, Bart.
Went to the masked ball as a fart.
He had painted his face
Like a more private place,
And his voice made the dowagers start.

1942A.

671

There was a young fellow named Bart
Who strained every shit through a fart.
Each tip-tapered turd
Was the very last word
In this deft and most intricate art.

1941.

672

There was a young man of Bhogat,
The cheeks of whose ass were so fat
That they had to be parted
Whenever he farted,
And propped wide apart when he shat.

1879-1941.

673

A cabman who drove in Biarritz
Once frightened a fare into fits.
When reprov'd for a fart,
He said, " God bless my heart,
When I break wind I usually shits. "

1879.

674

There was a young fellow named Brewster
Who said to his wife as he goosed her,
" It used to be grand
But just look at my hand;
You ain't wiping as clean as you used to. "

1942.

675

A nasty young joker named Bruce
Used to greet all his friends with a goose,
Till it came to a stop
In a handful of flop
From some bowels that were terribly loose.

1948A.

676

There was a fat lady of Bryde
Whose shoelaces once came untied.
She didn't dare stoop
For fear she would poop,
And she cried and she cried and she cried.

1927-1941.

677

There was a young man of Bulgaria
Who once went to piss down an area.
Said Mary to cook,
"Oh, do come and look,
Did you ever see anything hairier?"

1880.

678

There was a young friar of Byhill
Who went up to shit on a high hill.
When the abbot asked, "Was it
A goodly deposit?"
He said, "*Vox et praeterea nihil.*"

1941.

679

There was an old Bey of Calcutta
Who greased up his asshole with butter.
Instead of the roar
Which came there before,
Came a soft, oleaginous mutter.

1946B.

680

There once was a horse from Cape Verdes
Who produced most unusual turds,
By the simplest means
He'd eat corn and beans
And make succotash for the birds.

1947B.

681

A tourist who stopped at Capri
Was had by an old maid for tea.
When she wiggled he said,
As he patted her head,
" Ah, you're changing the 't' to a 'p'! "

1942A.

682

There was a young man named Cattell
Who knew psychophysics so well,
That each time he shit
He'd stop, measure it—
Its length, and its breadth, and its smell.

1939A.

683

An efficient young fellow named Cave
Said, " Think of the time that I save
By avoiding vacations
And sexy relations,
And taking a crap while I shave. "

1945.

684

There was a young fellow named Charted
Who rubbed soap on his bung when it smarted
And to his surprise
He received a grand prize,
For the bubbles he blew when he farted.

1941.

685

A nasty old bugger of Cheltenham
Once shit in his bags as he knelt in 'em.
So he sold 'em at Ware
To a gentleman there
Who didn't much like what he smelt in 'em.

1870.

686

There was a young fellow of Chiselhurst
Who never could piss till he'd whistle first.
One evening in June
He lost track of the tune—
Dum-da-de-dee... and his bladder burst!

1941.

687

There was a young fellow named Chivy
Who, whenever he went to the privy,
First solaced his mind,
And then wiped his behind,
With some well-chosen pages of Livy.

1946B.

688

Said the Duke to the Duchess of Chypre,
"Now, can-paper's grand for a wiper,
But I don't give a damn for
This new-fangled camphor-
and-menthol impregnated paper."

Said the Duchess, "Well yes, I daresay
Plain bum-wad's all right in its way,
But there's nothing so grand
As some leaves, or your hand,
When you're out in the woods for a day."

1941.

690

A young bio-chemist named Dan
Always followed his nose to the can.
He judged people best
By the urinal test,
As to race and to sex and to clan.

1941*

691

There was a faith-healer of Deal
Who said, "Although pain isn't real,
When, frightened by chance,
I unload in my pants,
I dislike what I fancy I feel."

1941.

692

There was an old person of Delhi
Awoke with a pain in his belly,
And to cure it, 'tis said,
He shit in his bed,
And the sheets were uncommonly smelly.

1870.

693

There was a young lady of Dexter
Whose husband exceedingly vexed her,
For whenever they'd start
He'd unfailingly fart
With a blast that damn nearly unsexed her.

1941.

694

There was a young lady of Dorset
Who went to an Underground closet.
She screwed up her ass
But passed only some gas,
And *that* wasn't tuppence-worth, was it?

1941.

695

There was a young woman named Dottie
Who said as she sat on her potty,
  "It isn't polite
    To do this in sight,
But then, who am I to be snotty?"

1946A.

696

My neighbors, the dirty Miss Drews,
Stand on their door-step and muse,
    And tie up their tresses
    While the dogs make their messes,
And I am wiping my shoes.

1936*

697

There was a young fellow of Ealing,
Devoid of all delicate feeling.
    When he read on the door:
  "Don't shit on the floor"
He jumped up and shat on the ceiling.

1941.

698

The Marquesa de Excusador
Used to pee on the drawing-room floor,
    For the can was so cold
    And when one grows old
To be much alone is a bore.

1942A.

699

While watching some tragical farces,
The audience had a catharsis.
    Instead of real tears
    They wept with their rears,
Which proves that catharsis my arse is.

1942-1951.

700

There was a young lady of Fismes
Who amazingly voided four streams.
　　A friend poked around
　　And a fly-button found
Wedged tightly in one of her seams.

1941.

701

There was a young lady from France
Supposed to play at a dance,
　　She ate a banana
　　And played the piano
And music came out of her pants.

1946A.

702

There was a young lady of Ghat
Who never could sit but she shat.
　　Oh, the seat of her drawers
　　Was a chamber of horrors,
And they felt even fouler than that!

1941.

703

There once was a fellow named Glantz
Who on entering a toilet in France,
　　Was in such a heat
　　To paper the seat,
He shit right into his pants.

1941*

704

Alas for a preacher named Hoke,
Whose shit was all stuck in his poke.
　　He farted a blast
　　That left hearers aghast,
But nothing emerged but some smoke.

1941.

705

A professor who taught at Holyoke
Had a bung like a red artichoke.
She was greatly annoyed
That each ripe haemorrhoid
Always quivered whenever she spoke.

1942A.

706

There once was a builder named Howell
Who had a remarkable bowel.
He built him a building
Of brickwork and gilding
Using—what do you think—on his trowel.

1947B.

707

That illustrious author, Dean Howells,
Had a terrible time with his bowels.
His wife, so they say,
Cleaned them out every day
With special elongated trowels.

1932.

708

Here's to the State of Iowa
Whose soil is soft and rich.
We need no turd
From your beautiful bird,*
You red headed son of a bitch.

1928A.

709

There was a young man from Kilbryde
Who fell in a shit house and died.
His heart-broken brother
Fell into another,
And now they're interred side by side.

1925*-1941.

710

There was a young girl of La Plata
Who was widely renowned as a farter.
Her deafening reports
At the Argentine sports
Made her much in demand as a starter.

1941.

711

Q. Flaccus in his third *liber*:
"The Romans have no wood-pulp fiber.
A crapulent quorum
Will squat in the Forum
And heave dirty stones in the Tiber."

1942A.

712

There was a young man of Loch Leven
Who went for a walk about seven.
He fell into a pit
That was brimful of shit,
And now the poor bugger's in heaven.

1928.

713

An old G.I. custom long-rooted
Is to entering fledglings well-suited.
In every latrine
A bright sign is seen:
"Stand close, the next guy may be barefooted."

1943.

714

There was a young Georgian named Lynd
Who'd never in all his life sinned,
For whenever he'd start
He'd be jarred by a fart,
And his semen was gone with the wind.

1941.

715

There was a young man named McBride
Who could fart whenever he tried.
In a contest he blew
Two thousand and two,
And then shit and was disqualified.

1945C.

716

There was a young man named McFee
Who was stung in the balls by a bee.
He made oodles of money
By oozing pure honey
Every time he attempted to pee.

1943A.

717

There was a young girl of Machias
Whose bloomers were cut on the bias,
With an opening behind
To let out the wind,
And to let the boys in once or twias.

1938.

718

There was a young fellow named Malcolm
Who dusted his ass-hole with talcum.
He'd always use it
Every time that he shit,
And found the sensation right welcome.

1943.

719

There was an old man of Madrid
Who went to an auction to bid.
In the first lot they sold
Was an ancient commode—
And, my god, when they lifted the lid!

1941.

720

There was a young Royal Marine
Who tried to fart "God Save the Queen."
When he reached the soprano
Out came the guano,
And his breeches weren't fit to be seen.

1879-1928.

721

There is a professor named Martin
From whom I'm about to be partin',
And on my way out
He may hear me shout,
"It's your face I'd sure like to fart in."

1943.

722

A movement once rose 'mongst the masses
To travel about with bare asses.
At true lovers' parting
The best form was farting,
With buttocks immersed in molasses.

1941*

723

A gay young blade from Milano
Was Count Galeazzo Ciano.
Safe from the wars,
He found that his drawers
Contained rich deposits of guano.

1946B.

724

There once was a lady named Muir
Whose mind was so frightfully pure
That she fainted away
At a friend's house one day
When she saw some canary manure.

1939A.

725

There was a young lady of Newcastle
Who wrapped up a turd in a parcel,
And sent it to a relation
With this invitation—
" It has just come out hot from my arsehole. "

1870.

726

There was an old scholar named Nick
Who wrote Latin and Greek with his prick.
He peed a paean
In the snow by a john
In script more than three inches thick.

1941.

727

An eminent preacher named Nixon
Used to fart as he said benediction.
The shy flock would smile
As they trooped down the aisle :
" The arse on our parson needs fixin'. "

1942A.

728

There was a young girl in Ohio
Whose baptismal name was Maria.
She would put on airs
And pee on the stairs,
If she thought that no one was nigh 'er.

1927.

729

There was a young lady of Pinner,
Who dreamt that her lover was in her.
This excited her heart,
So she let a great fart,
And shit out her yesterday's dinner.

1870.

730

There was an old man who could piss
Through a ring—and, what's more, never miss.
People came by the score,
And bellowed, "Encore!
Won't you do it again, Sir? Bis! Bis!"

1928.

731

There was a young lady of Purdbright
Who never could quite get her turd right.
She'd go to the closet
And leave a deposit
Like a mouse or a bat or a bird might.

1941.

732

There was an old fellow of Pittwood
Who never was able to shit good.
He'd leave small deposits
On shelves and in closets,
As a very small pup or a kit would.

1949.

733

There was a young man of Rangoon
Whose farts could be heard to the moon.
When least you'd expect 'em,
They'd burst from his rectum
With the force of a raging typhoon.

1941.

734

There was a young man of Rangoon
Who farted and filled a balloon.
The balloon went so high
That it stuck in the sky,
And stank out the Man in the Moon.

1879.

735

There was an old fellow from Roop
Who'd lost all control of his poop.
  One evening at supper
  His wife said, " Now, Tupper,
Stop making that noise with your soup! "

1927-1941.

736

The intestines of Dante Rossetti
Were exceedingly fragile and petty.
  All he could eat
  Was finely chopped meat,
And all he could shit was spaghetti.

1932.

737

There was a young man from St. Paul
Who had really no scruples at all—
  He would fart when he'd talk,
  And shit when he'd walk,
And at night throw it over the wall.

1943-1952.

738

There was an old soldier named Schmitt
Took a trip to the can for to shit.
  To his epic despair
  No paper was there,
So he simply continued to sit.

1943-1951.

739

Tom, Tom, the piper's son,
Let loose a fart, and away he run.
  But Tom fell in
  An old shit bin
And ever since then Tom stinks like sin!

1941*

740. THE FARTER FROM SPARTA

There was a young fellow from Sparta,
A really magnificent farter,
    On the strength of one bean
    He'd fart God Save the Queen,
And Beethoven's Moonlight Sonata.

He could vary, with proper persuasion,
His fart to suit any occasion.
    He could fart like a flute,
    Like a lark, like a lute,
This highly fartistic Caucasian.

This sparkling young farter from Sparta,
His fart for no money would barter.
    He could roar from his rear
    Any scene from Shakespeare,
Or Gilbert and Sullivan's Mikado.

He'd fart a gavotte for a starter,
And fizzle a fine serenata.
    He could play on his anus
    The Coriolanus:
Oof, boom, er-tum, tootle, yum tah-dah!

He was great in the Christmas Cantata,
He could double-stop fart the Toccata,
    He'd boom from his ass
    Bach's B-Minor Mass,
And in counterpoint, La Traviata.

Spurred on by a very high wager
With an envious German named Bager,
He'd proceeded to fart
The complete oboe part
Of a Haydn Octet in B-major.

His repertoire ranged from classics to jazz,
He achieved new effects with bubbles of gas.
With a good dose of salts
He could whistle a waltz
Or swing it in razzamatazz.

His basso profundo with timbre so rare
He rendered quite often, with power to spare.
But his great work of art,
His fortissimo fart,
He saved for the Marche Militaire.

One day he was dared to perform
The William Tell Overture Storm,
But naught could dishearten
Our spirited Spartan,
For his fart was in wonderful form.

It went off in capital style,
And he farted it through with a smile,
Then, feeling quite jolly,
He tried the finale,
Blowing double-stopped farts all the while.

The selection was tough, I admit,
But it did not dismay him one bit,
    Then, with ass thrown aloft
    He suddenly coughed...
And collapsed in a shower of shit.

His bunghole was blown back to Sparta,
Where they buried the rest of our farter,
    With a gravestone of turds
    Inscribed with the words:
"To the Fine Art of Farting, A Martyr."

1938-1948A.

752

The damned Jap sons-a-bitches,
We made them wet their britches.
    We grabbed our gun,
    And made 'em run,
The goddamned sons-a-bitches.

1943*

753

There was a young man from Split
Who was thrilled with the thought of a shit.
    He was simply elated,
    Till he grew constipated,
But that took all the pleasure from it.

1943.

754

A keen-scented dean of Tacoma
Was awarded a special diploma
    For his telling apart
    Of a masculine fart
From a similar female aroma.

1947.

755

I sat by the Duchess at tea,
And she asked, "Do you fart when you pee?"
I said with some wit,
"Do you belch when you shit?"
And felt it was one up for me.

1928-1941.

756

When asked by the Duchess at tea
If an eggplant I ever did see,
I said "Yes," rather bored;
She said, "Sir, you've explored
Up a hen's ass much further than me."

1946B.

757

There was a young man from Ti' Juana
Who declared as he wallowed in guano,
"It may seem imbecilic
To be *so* coprophilic—
I indulge in it just 'cause I wanna."

1948A.

758

There was a young fellow named Twyss
Whose orgasms forced him to piss,
And most girls objected
To having injected
A flood of his piss 'midst their bliss.

But one girl—a smart little floozie—
Saw reason for being less choosey.
Said this sensible miss,
"Well, anyway, Chris,
Your piss certn'y cleans out my coosie."

1941.

760

"It's true," confessed Jane, Lady Torres,
"That often I beg lifts in lorries.
When the men stop to piss
I see things that I miss
When I travel alone in my Morris."

1947A.

761

There once was a sailor from Wales,
An expert at pissing in gales.
He could piss in a jar
From the top-gallant spar
Without even wetting the sails.

1941.

762

There was an old lady from Wheeling
Who had a peculiar feeling,
She laid on her back
And opened her crack
And pissed all over the ceiling.

1870-1925*

763

There was an old lady of Ypres
Who got shot in the ass by some snipers,
And when she blew air
Through the holes that were there,
She astonished the Cameron Pipers.

1941.

IX

GOURMANDS

764

There was a young sapphic named Anna
Who stuffed her friend's cunt with banana,
Which she sucked bit by bit
From her partner's warm slit,
In the most approved lesbian manner.

1934-1941.

765

There was a young girl of Antietam
Who liked horse turds so well she could eat 'em
She'd lie on their rumps
And swallow the lumps
As fast as the beasts could excrete 'em.

1947B.

766

There was a young man had the art
Of making a capital tart
With a handful of shit,
Some snot and a spit,
And he'd flavor the whole with a fart.

1879.

767

There was an old man of Balbriggan,
Who cunt juice was frequently swigging,
But even to this
He preferred tom-cat's piss,
Which he kept a pox'd nigger to frig in.

1879.

768

There once was a midget named Carr
Who couldn't reach up to the bar,
So in every saloon
He climbed a spittoon,
And guzzled his liquor from thar.

1939A.

769

There was a young man from the coast
Who ate melted shit on his toast.
When the toast saw the shit
It collapsed in a fit,
For the shit was its grandfather's ghost.

1934.

770

There was an old man of Corfu
Who fed upon cunt-juice and spew.
When he couldn't get that,
He ate what he shat—
And bloody good shit he shat, too.

On clinkers his choice often fell,
Or clabbered piss brought to a jell.
When these palled to his taste
He tried snot and turd-paste,
And found them delicious as well.

He ate them, and sighed, and said, "What
Uncommonly fine shit and snot!
Now really, the two
Are too good to be true—
I would rather have et them than not."

1879-1941.

773

A Dutchman who dwelt in Dundee
Walked in to a grocer's named Lee.
He said, " If you blease,
Haff you any prick cheese ? "
Said the grocer, " I'll skin back and see. "

1941-1948.

774

A coprophagous fellow named Fleam
Loved to drink a strong urinal stream.
He seduced little gonsils
Into spraying his tonsils
With the stuff he liked best on earth : cream.

1942.

775

There was a young fellow named Fritz
Who planted an acre of tits.
They came up in the fall,
Pink nipples and all,
And he chewed them all up into bits.

1941.

776

There was a young man of Glengarridge,
The fruit of a scrofulous marriage.
He sucked off his brother,
And buggered his mother,
And ate up his sister's miscarriage.

1934-1941.

777

A daughter of fair Ioway,
While at sport in the toilet one day,
Swallowed some of her pee,
"And hereafter, " said she,
" I'll do it at lunch every day. "

1946A.

778

A young lady who once had a Jew beau
Found out soon that he'd got a bubo,
So when it was ripe
She put in a pipe,
And sucked up the juice through a tube oh!

1870.

779

There was a young fellow of Kent
Who had a peculiar bent.
He collected the turds
Of various birds,
And had them for lunch during Lent.

1947B.

780

There was a young man of King's Cross
Who amused himself frigging a horse,
Then licking the spend
Which still dripped from the end,
Said, "It tastes just like anchovy sauce."

1879.

781

A hypocritical bastard named Legman
When drinking piss-highballs puts egg in 'em.
If he tells you you're queer
To enjoy pissless beer,
Just say to him, "Quit pulling my leg, man!"

1952.

782

There was a young fellow from Leith
Who used to skin cocks with his teeth.
It wasn't for pleasure
He adopted this measure,
But to get at the cheese underneath.

1934-1938.

783

Said a busy young whore known as Mable,
Who at fucking was willing and able,
" It's a pity to waste
All that juicy white paste, "
So she served it in bowls at the table.

1942.

784

There once was a U.S. marine
Whose manners were slightly obscene.
He loved to eat jizz,
Both others' and his,
When served in a hot soup-tureen.

1941*

785

There was a young man from Marseilles
Who lived on clap juice and snails.
When tired of these
He lived upon cheese
From his prick, which he picked with his nails.

1927.

786

There was an old maid from Shalot
Who lived upon frog shit and snot.
When she tired of these
She would eat the green cheese
That she scraped from the sides of her twat.

1927-1943C.

787

There was an old sailor named Jock
Who was wrecked on a desolate rock.
He had nothing to eat
But the punk of his feet,
And the cheese from the end of his cock.

1941.

788

There once was a baker of Nottingham
Who in making éclairs would put snot in 'em.
When he ran out of snot,
He would, like as not,
Take his pecker and jack off a shot in 'em.

1941.

789

There was a young fellow of Perth,
The nastiest bastard on earth,
When his wife was confined
He pulled down the blind,
And ate up the whole afterbirth.

1941.

790

A mannerly fellow named Phyfe
Was greatly distressed by his wife,
For whene'er she was able
She'd shit on the table,
And gobble the shit—with her knife!

1944A.

791

There were two little mice in Rangoon
Who sought lunch in an old lady's womb.
Cried one mouse, "By Jesus,
I'll wager this cheese is
As old as the cheese in the moon!"

1941.

792

Where was a young lady of Rheims
Who was terribly plagued with wet dreams.
She saved up a dozen,
And sent to her cousin,
Who ate them and thought they were creams.

1879.

793

An elderly rabbi named Riskin
Dines daily on cunt-juice and foreskin.
    And to further his bliss,
    At dessert he'll drink piss,
For which he is always a'thirstin'.

1946A.

794

There was a young man known as Royce
Who took an emetic by choice.
    He was fed, quite by chance,
    Half the crotch of the pants
Of a girl who kept crab-lice as toys.

1942-1952.

795

There was a young man of St. Just
Who ate of new bread till he bust.
    It was not the crumb,
    For that passed through his bum,
But what buggered him up was the crust.

1870.

796

There was an old man of Seringapatam
Besmeared his wife's anus with raspberry jam,
    Then licked off the sweet,
    And pronounced it a treat,
And for public opinion he cared not a damn.

1870.

797

There was a young lady of Totten
Whose tastes grew perverted and rotten.
    She cared not for steaks,
    Or for pastry and cakes,
But lived upon penis *au gratin*.

1938.

798

There was a young man of the Tweed
Who sucked his wife's arse thro' a reed.
When she had diarrhoea
He'd let none come near,
For fear they should poach on his feed.

1879.

799

There was a young pair from Uganda
Who were having a fuck on a veranda.
The drip from their fucks
Fed forty-two ducks,
Three geese, and a fucking big gander.

1942.

800

A hungry old trollop from Yemen
Did a pretty good business with he-men.
But she gave up all fucking
In favor of sucking,
For the protein contained in the semen.

1947B.

X

VIRGINITY

801

Sass Mädelein unter den Aestchen
Und spielt' mit dem Knäbleinmästchen,
　　Dem niedlichen Zweck—
　　Bald ist der Kranz weg:
Blieb nichts davon nur das Kästchen.

1942A.

802

A maiden sat under a tree
And played with the lad's fiddle-dee,
　　His little wood post—
　　Soon her jewel is lost
From the casket where it used to be.

1942A.

803

"Competition is keen, you'll agree,"
Said an ancient old flapper from Dee,
　　So she dyed her gray tresses,
　　Chopped a foot from her dresses,
And her *reason* you plainly can see.

1927.

804

The bride went up the aisle
In traditional virginal style,
　　But they say she was nary
　　An innocent cherry,
But a whore from the banks of the Nile.

1948A.

805

There was a young virgin named Alice
Who thought of her cunt as a chalice.
    One night, sleeping nude,
    She awoke feeling lewd,
And found in her chalice a phallus.

1941.

806

There was a young lady of Andover,
And the boys used to ask her to hand over
    Her sexual favor,
    Which she did (may God save her!)
For her morals she had no command over.

1951.

807

There was a young girl named Anheuser
Who said that no man could surprise her.
    But Pabst took a chance,
    Found Schlitz in her pants,
And now she is sadder Budweiser.

1927-1932.

808

To the shrine which was Pallas Athena's
Young Bito (who'd learned about penis)
    Brought her needles and thread
    And scissors and said,
"You can stick them—I'm changing to Venus!"

1942A.

809

There's a tiresome young girl in Bay Shore,
When her fiancé cried, "I adore
    Your beautiful twat!"
    She replied, "Like as not—
It's pretty, but what is it *for*?"

1952.

810

There once was a tart named Belinda
Whose cunt opened out like a window.
    But she'd slam the thing shut,
    The contemptible slut,
Whenever you tried to get inda.

1941.

811

A lisping young lady named Beth
Was saved from a fate worse than death
    Seven times in a row,
    Which unsettled her so
That she quit saying "No" and said "Yeth."

1943A.

812

There was a young lady of Bhore
Who was courted by gallants galore.
    Their ardent protestin'
    She found interestin',
And ended her life as a virgin.

1943A.

813

There was a young fellow named Biddle
Whose girl had to teach him to fiddle.
    She grabbed hold of his bow
    And said, " If you want to know,
You can try parting my hair in the middle."

1942.

814

In Stokes lived an ugly bluestocking
Who declared the men's manners were shocking.
    Why, she'd never been diddled,
    Even fingered or fiddled...
So she finally moved over to Focking.

1942A.

815

There was a young virgin of Bude
Whose tricks, though exciting, were viewed
With distrust by the males
For she'd fondle their rails,
But never would let them intrude.

1941.

816

There was an old spinster named Campbell
Got tangled one day in a bramble.
She cried, "Ouch, how it sticks!
But so many sharp pricks
Are not met every day on a ramble."

1942.

817

There was a young girl from the Cape
Who filled her hole with bicycle tape
To ease up the pangs
Caused by the whangs
Of gentlemen bent upon rape.

1939A.

818

There was a young Miss from Cape Cod
Who at soldiers would not even nod.
But she tripped in a ditch
And some son-of-a-bitch
Of a corporal raped her, by God!

1928B-1943A.

819

There once was a passionate Celte
Who'd an urge to know how a cock felt.
One went in, hard and straight,
But her heat was so great
That she found she had caused it to melt.

1941.

820

A Salvation Lassie named Claire
Was having her first love affair.
    As she climbed into bed
    She reverently said,
"I wish to be opened with prayer."

1943A.

821

An innocent maiden of Clewer
Incited her boy-friend to screw her.
    She tried to say no,
    A half-second slow—
Now when she sits down she says, "Oo-er!"

1952.

822

There was a young lady of Corbie
Who said, "Oh, the men really bore me!
    But I reckon, without 'em,
    Though I hate 'em and scout 'em,
There just would be no one to scour me."

1952.

823

There was a young lady of Crewe
Whose cherry a chap had got through,
    Which she told to her mother
    Who fixed her another
Out of rubber and red ink and glue.

1941.

824

There was a young princess called Dagmar
Who said, "I should so like to shag, Ma,"
    And says she, "If you speaks
    To the King of the Greeks,
He will lend me his own tolliwag, Ma."

1870.

825

There was a young girl of Dalkeith
With a hymen in need of relief,
So she went to the doctor
Who prodded and shocked her,
And stretched it with fingers and teeth.

1952.

826

A girl named Alice, in Dallas,
Had never felt of a phallus.
She remained virgo intacto,
Because, ipso facto,
No phallus in Dallas fit Alice.

1946B.

827

An ignorant virgin of Dee
Entertained a man's cock just to see
If the darn thing would fit—
It went off in her pit,
And she cried, "Hey! that's no place to pee!"

1941.

828

A young lady who taught at Devizes
Was had up at the local assizes
For teaching young boys
Matrimonial joys,
And giving French letters as prizes.

1941.

829

A complacent old don of Divinity
Made boast of his daughter's virginity.
They must have been dawdlin'
Down at old Magdalen—
It couldn't have happened at Trinity.

1938.

830

There was a young virgin of Dover
Who was raped in the woods by a drover.
When the going got hard
He greased her with lard,
Which felt nice, so they started all over.

1941.

831

There was a young girl of East Lynne
Whose mother, to save her from sin,
Had filled up her crack
To the brim with shellac,
But the boys picked it out with a pin.

1927-1941.

832

The first love of a lady named Ederle
Found her hymen obstructed him steadily,
But he merely rubbed lard on
The end of his hard on,
And then found he entered quite readily.

1941.

833

There was a bluestocking in Florence
Wrote anti-sex pamphlets in torrents,
Till a Spanish grandee
Got her off with his knee,
And she burned all her works with abhorrence.

1942A.

834

A homely old spinster of France,
Who all the men looked at askance,
Threw her skirt overhead
And then jumped into bed,
Saying, " Now I've at least half a chance. "

1941.

835. THE MISFORTUNES OF FYFE

There was a young fellow named Fyfe
Who married the pride of his life,
    But imagine his pain
    When he struggled in vain,
And just couldn't get into his wife.

Now the trouble was not with our hero,
Who, though no match for Epstein or Nero,*
    Had a good little dong
    That was five inches long,
And as stiff as a parsnip at zero.

But his efforts to poke her, assiduous,
Met a dense growth of hair most prodiguous.
    Well, he thought he might dint her
    By waiting till winter,
But he found that she wasn't deciduous.

Now here was this fellow named Fyfe,
Unable to diddle his wife—
    Which fact, sad but true,
    Left him nothing to do
But bugger the girl all his life.

For diversion this might have been funny,
And of course it *did* save him some money,
    But it angered our Fyfey
    To think that his wifey
Was hoarding her deep nest of honey.

He went whoring to find satisfaction,
But with whores, though accomplished in action,
    He never could capture
    That fine fucking rapture,
For the thought of his wife was distraction.

So here was our fellow named Fyfe
With a truly impervious wife.
    She was not worth a damn,
    Being close as a clam—
Why, he couldn't get in with a knife!

The problem that harassed his soul
Was : what kept him out of her hole?
    Was her hymen too tough?
    Was she stuffed up with fluff?
Was her coosie the home of a mole?

This was just what poor Fyfe couldn't tell,
For her prow was as sound as a bell.
    He'd have needed a gimlet
    To get into her quimlet,
And it made the poor guy mad as hell.

He applied to that fellow from Strensall
For help from his long, pointed pencil,
    But Strensy's tool now
    Was as blunt as the prow
Of a tug—he'd have needed a stencil.

Fyfe searched for the chap from New York
Who had punctured the hymen like cork,
    But *he* was quite coy
    For he now loved a boy,
And refused to help Fyfe with the stork.

Fyfe asked Durand how much he'd charge
(The fellow whose cock could contract or enlarge)
    To drill his way in
    With his prick like a pin,
And there make it slowly enlarge.

But Durand—though he'd fuck with no urgin'—
Warned, "Apart from the risk that she'll burgeon,
    Your pride must be low
    If you'll meekly forego
A crack at a genuine virgin."

In the spring in the woods Fyfe did wander late,
And saw couples preparing to copulate,
    But he could not abide
    The gay sight, and he cried
At the thought that the pigfuckers penetrate!

One couple he foolishly leapt on,
To examine the wound and the weapon.
    One was rigid, one deep—
    The snug fit made him weep,
And in shame and contrition he crept on.

In the meantime, Fyfe's wife, who had wed
With *some* thought to the pleasures of bed,
    Was becoming depressed,
    In fact damn near obsessed
By her terribly tough maidenhead.

She remarked, " When all joking is done,
What I honestly want is a son.
    I would like impregnation
    If not copulation—
But to wed and have neither's no fun. "

She grew worried and nervous and thin,
Till Fyfe said, " You would jump at a pin! "
    And these words, though unkind,
    Put the thought in her mind
That a pin-point *perhaps* might get in.

Thus she thought of synthetic conception,
Which at first seemed like basest deception,
    But her cunt was so sore
    From Fyfe's trying to bore,
That she gave the thought better reception.

And indeed, though it's sad to relate it,
Her first fuck was so sadly belated,
    That a poke by a pin,
    Though ever so thin,
Was a prospect that made her elated.

To be brief, the great action was done:
There was artfully planted, a son,
  Through a bodkin that filled her,
  And wonderfully thrilled her—
More fun than a son of a gun!

This syringe, which was long but quite thin,
Left a hole that Fyfe couldn't get in,
  But he kept right on busting
  And jousting and thrusting,
On account of his excess of vim.

While she mused on this synthetic screw,
The sperm got well-planted, and grew,
  And the great day approached
  When her breech would be broached,
But Fyfe, the poor wretch, never knew.

One night, while in sheer desperation
He prodded and poked like tarnation,
  His wife groaned with pain—
  She gave way!! Would he gain
The goal of three years' contemplation?

The head of his dingus went in!
He felt sure he was going to win!
  He thrust like a demon,
  He spilt all his semen,
And scraped off a square inch of skin.

But despite all his trying, he found
He was losing, not gaining, his ground.
    Though he clung to her thighs
    While he tried for the prize,
Each push *in* caused a greater rebound.

The harder the poor fellow tried,
The more her hold filled, from inside,
    Till he fell back quite spent,
    His prick battered and bent,
And a few minutes later—he died.

As he passed, a new life was begun,
And his tomb tells how he was undone:
  "Shed a tear for poor Fyfe,
    His imperforate wife
Did him in with the aid of their son."

1938-1941.

863

A neuropath-virgin named Flynn
Shouted before she gave in:
  "It isn't the deed,
    Or the fear of the seed,
But that big worm that's shedding its skin!"

1942A.

864

There was a young fellow named Gluck
Who found himself shit out of luck.
    Though he petted and wooed,
    When he tried to get screwed
He found virgins just don't give a fuck.

1941.

865

There was an old spinster named Gretel
Who wore underclothes made of metal.
When they said, " Does it hurt? "
She said, " It keeps dirt
From stamen and pistil and petal. "

1942.

866

There were three young ladies of Grimsby
Who said, "Of what use can our quims be?
The hole in the middle
Is so we can piddle,
But for what can the hole in the rims be?"

1928-1938.

867

There was a young lady of Harwich
Who said on the morn of her marriage,
" I shall sew my chemise
Right down to my knees,
For I'm damned if I fuck in the carriage! "

1880.

868

I don't mind if a girl rides a hel'copter,
I don't mind if a girl rides a car,
But the girl who rides straddle
An old fashioned saddle
Is stretching things a bit too far.

1945C.

869

There was a young girl from Hoboken
Who claimed that her hymen was broken
From riding a bike
On a cobblestone pike,
But it really was broken from pokin'.

1945.

870

There was a young brave who got hot
And chased an old squaw who was not.
So she stuffed her canal
With some dried chapparal,
And sprinkled some sand on her twat.

1942A.

871

A lady of virginal humours
Would only be screwed through her bloomers.
But one fatal day
The bloomers gave way,
Which fixed her for future consumers.

1941.

872

A girl who lived in Kentucky
Said, " Yes, I've been awfully lucky.
No man ever yet
On my back made me get,
But sometimes I feel awful fucky."

1927.

873

Exclaimed a young girl in Kildare,
As her lover's jock towered in air,
" If that goes in me I
Shall certainly die—
As I shall if it does not go there."

1942A.

874

There was an old lady of Leicester,
And no man had ever caressed her,
And all day she'd wriggle
And giggle and jiggle,
As though seven devils possessed her.

1941.

875

A coon who was out with his Liz
Said, "Baby, let's get down to biz."
Said she, "That cain't be,
Less you'se stronger'n me,
But, honey, I reckon you is."

1927.

876

There was a young girl named McKnight
Who got drunk with her boy-friend one night.
She came to in bed
With a split maidenhead—
That's the last time she ever was tight.

1941.

877

That Jew-girl, the famed Virgin Mary,
Said, "Oh God, my quim's got all hairy!
To hell with virginity,
I'll fuck the whole Trinity!
I'm tired of vice solitary."

1943B-1944A.

878

No one can tell about Myrtle
Whether she's sterile or fertile.
If anyone tries
To tickle her thighs
She closes them tight like a turtle.

1943.

879

There was a young widow of Nain
Who the bedclothes did frequently stain,
With such great inflammation
Came such menstruation,
Her cunt so long idle had lain.

1870.

880

A certain young sheik I'm not namin'
Asked a flapper he thought he was tamin',
"Have you your maidenhead?"
"Don't be foolish," she said,
"But I still have the box that it came in."

1948.

881

There is a young girl from New York
Who is cautious from fear of the stork.
You will find she is taped
To prevent being raped,
And her ass-hole is plugged with a cork.

1947-1951.

882

There was a young girl of Ostend
Who her maidenhead tried to defend,
But a Chasseur d'Afrique
Inserted his prick
And taught that ex-maid how to spend.

1879.

883

There was a young fellow from Oudh
Whose mind was excessively lewd.
He asserted, "All women
Seen dancin' or swimmin'
Would rather be home gettin' screwed."

1949.

884

A girl at whom no one made passes
No longer resents wearing glasses,
For two F.B.I. men
Demolished her hymen
On failing to find her New Masses.

1949.

885

There was a young virgin in Perth
Swore she'd do it for no one on earth,
Yet she fell without scandal
To a red Christmas candle
And was always less choosey henceforth.

1942A.

886

There was an old maid in Peru
Who'd a dog and a cat and a gnu.
From a sailor named Harrot
She bought an old parrot,
And he threw in a young cockatoo.

1941.

887

There was a young lassie named Phyllis
Was deflowered one night in a Willys.
Before they were through
Her spine was askew,
And I very much fear that it still is.

1943A.

888

A Newfoundland lad from Placentia
Was in love to the point of dementia,
But his love couldn't burgeon
With his touch-me-not virgin
'Til he screwed her by hand in absentia.

1947B.

889

There was a young lady from 'Quoddie
Who had a magnificent body,
And her face was not bad,
Yet she'd never been had
For her odor was markèdly coddy.

1949.

890

A pathetic appellant at Reno
Was as chaste as the holy Bambino,
For she'd married a slicker
Who stuck to his liquor
And scorned her ripe maraschino.

1947B.

891

There was a young man of St. Kitt
Who was screwing a spinster, but quit.
Said she, " Don't be scary,
It's only my cherry, "
But he said, " It feels more like a pit. "

1941.

892

There was a young girl of Samoa
Who determined that no man should know her.
One young fellow tried
But she wriggled aside,
And spilled all the spermatozoa.

1928-1932.

893

Maggie is such a sad sack of shit
That no one will tickle her tit.
It would make her so glad
To be had by a lad,
Her drawers cream at the mere thought of it.

1943.

894

There was a young fellow named Simon
Who tried to discover a hymen,
But he found every girl
Had relinquished her pearl
In exchange for a solitaire diamond.

1941.

895

There was a T/5, name of Snyder,
Who took out a girl just to ride her.
 She allowed him to feel
 From her neck to her heel,
But never would let him inside her.

1943.

896

There was a young girl from Sofia
Who succumbed to her lover's desire.
 She said, "It's a sin,
 But now that it's in,
Could you shove it a few inches higher?"

1945.

897

There was a young girl of Spitzbergen
Whose people all thought her a virgin,
 Till they found her in bed
 With her quim very red,
And the head of a kid just emergin'.

1928.

898

An innocent soldier named Stave
Was almost seduced by a Wave.
 But he's still a recluse
 With all of his juice,
For he didn't know how to behave.

1944.

899

There was a young fellow named Sweeney
Whose girl was a terrible meanie.
 The hatch of her snatch
 Had a catch that would latch—
She could only be screwed by Houdini.

1941.

900

A proper young lady of Taos
Had her panties trimmed neatly with lace.
But a vulgar young man
Raped her roughly, and ran,
And left them pure panties in chaos.

1941.

901

There was a young girl of Topeka
Who from diddling grew weaker and weaker,
Till a guy, name of Dick,
Went and offered his prick,
So she tried it and shouted, " Eureka! "

1951.

902

There was an old spinster of Tyre
Who bellowed, " My cunt is on fire! "
So a fireman was found,
Brought his engine around,
And extinguished her burning desire.

1941.

903

There was an old maid in Van Nuys
Who went crazy from making mud pies.
She would fill them with farts
And pickled beef-hearts,
And bake them between her fierce thighs.

1942A.

904

There was a young girl named Venus
Who had never encountered a penis.
When Van Stone threw his in
It went up to her chin,
But the bore, not the stroke, was the meanest.

1945C.

905

A skinny old maid from Verdun
Wed a short-peckered son-of-a-gun.
She said, "I don't care
If there isn't much there.
God knows it is better than none."

1927-1932.

906

There was a young virgin named Violet
Whose hope was to remain inviolate.
But she let a man neck her
And soon his hard pecker
Had wedged itself firmly in Violet.

1941*

907

There was a young lady named Wilma
Who said, "Oh now, please do not kilma.
I love your advances
And what's in your pantses,
Do you think it could possibly fill-ma?"

1951.

908

There was a young lady of Worcester
Who dreamt that a rooster seduced her.
She woke with a scream,
But 'twas only a dream—
A bump in the mattress had goosed her.

1932-1941.

909

There was a young lady called Wylde,
Who kept herself quite undefiled
By thinking of Jesus,
Contagious diseases,
And the bother of having a child.

1927-1928.

XI

MOTHERHOOD

910

There once was a Vassar B.A.
Who pondered the problem all day
    Of what there would be
    If C-U-N-T
Were divided by C-O-C-K.

A young Ph.D. passing by,
She gave him the problem to try.
    He worked the division
    With perfect precision,
And the answer was B-A-B-Y.

1928A-1941.

912

To a widow-bereaved of Barrientos
Her marital divertimentos
    Are so sentimental—
    Even things contraceptal,
That old fishskins are dearest mementos.

1944A.

913

There was a young girl who begat
Three brats, by name Nat, Pat, and Tat.
    It was fun in the breeding
    But hell in the feeding,
When she found there was no tit for Tat.

1941.

914

There was a young girl of Bombay
Who was put in the family way
　By the mate of a lugger,
　An ignorant bugger
Who always spelled CUNT with a K.

1927-1941.

915

An indolent vicar of Bray
Kept his wife in the family way,
　Till she grew more alert,
　Bought a vaginal squirt,
And said to her spouse, "Let us spray!"

1941.

916

There was a young man of Cape Cod
Who once put my wife into pod.
　His name it was Tucker
　The dirty old fucker,
The bugger, the blighter, the sod!

1927.

917

There was a young man of Cape Horn
Who wished he had never been born.
　And he wouldn't have been
　If his father had seen
That the end of the rubber was torn.

1927-1928.

918

There was a young pessimist, Grotton,
Who wished he had ne'er been begotten,
　Nor would he have been
　But the rubber was thin,
And right at the tip it was rotten.

1941.

919

There once was a modern young chick
Who wished above all to be chic.
She thought it much neater
(Not to mention discreeter)
To do it with a sheik with a " Sheik."

1942.

920

There was a young girl of Claridge's
Who said, " What a strange thing marriage is,
When you stop to think
That I've poured down the sink
Five abortions and fifty miscarriages! "

1943B.

921

There was an old lady, God damn her,
She fucked herself with a hammer.
The hammer was blunt
And so was her cunt,
And out came a kid with a hop, skip, and jump.

1928B.

922

There was a young lady of Delhi
Who had a bad pain in her belly.
Her relations all smiled
C'os they found her with child
By his honour the C—f B—n K—y.

1870.

923

There was a young girl whose divinity
Preserved her in perfect virginity,
'Til a candle, her nemesis,
Caused parthenogenesis—
Now she thinks herself one of the Trinity.

1943A.

924

A pious young lady named Finnegan
Would caution her beau, " Now you're in again,
Please watch it just right
So you'll last through the night,
For I certainly don't want to sin again. "

1941.

925

There was a young girl from the five-and-ten
Who diddled herself with a fountain pen.
The top came off,
The ink went wild,
And now she's the mother of a colored child.

1928A-1941.

926

There was a young lady named Flo
Whose lover had pulled out too slow.
So they tried it all night
Till he got it just right...
Well, practice makes pregnant, you know.

1941.

927

There was a young lady of France
Who went to the Palace to dance.
She danced with a Turk
Till he got in his dirk,
And now she can't button her pants.

1941.

928

There once was a midwife of Gaul,
Who had hardly no business at all.
She cried, " Hell and damnation!
There's no procreation—
God made the French penis too small. "

1941.

929

My wife Myrtle's womb has a habit
Of expanding whenever I stab it.
What's more, my wife Myrtle
Is so wondrously fertile,
That she's giving me kids like a rabbit.

1944.

930

There once was a handsome Haitian,
The luckiest dog in creation.
He worked for the rubber trust
Teaching the upper crust
The science of safe copulation.

1941.

931

There was a young lady named Hall
Who went to a birth-control ball.
She was loaded with pessaries
And other accessories,
But no one approached her at all.

1938.

932

A medical student named Hetrick
Is learnèd in matters obstetric.
From a glance at the toes
Of the mother, he knows
If the fetus's balls are symmetric.

1943.

933

Old King Cole was a bugger for the hole,
And a bugger for the hole was he.
He called for his wife
And stuck her with a knife,
And out jumped a K-I-D.

1925*

934

There was a young man of Jesus
Who performed cheap abortions with tweezers.
One night in a hunt
Up a mummified cunt
He found a F. L. of Caesar's.

1941-1947B.

935

There was a young lady of Louth
Who suddenly grew very stout.
Her mother said, "Nelly,
There's more in your belly
Than ever went in through your mouth."

1928-1941.

936

There was a young lady from Thrace
Whose corsets got too tight to lace.
Her mother said, "Nelly,
There's things in your belly
That never got in through your face."

1932-1950.

937

Frankie and Johnny were lovers
Especially under the covers.
When she pulled out his trigger
She said, "Mmm, what a figger!
But it makes so many girls mothers."

1942.

938

There was a young girl of Madrid
Who thought she'd be having a kid.
So by holding her water
Three months and a quarter
She drowned the poor bastard, she did.

1941.

939. REDWING

There once was an Indian Maid,
A whore she was by trade,
For two-bits a whack
She'd lay on her back,
And let the cowboys ram it up her crack.

One day to her surprise
Her belly began to rise,
And out of her jigger
Jumped a cast-iron nigger
With balls between his eyes.

Oh, the moon shines tonight on Mrs. Porter,
She had a daughter
Who was a slaughterer,
She washed her cunt with caustic soda
To keep the odor
From growing strong.

1935*

942

There was a young lady of Maine
Who declared she'd a man on the brain.
But you knew from the view
Of the way her waist grew,
It was not on her brain that he'd lain.

1941.

943

There was an old whore of Marseilles
Who tried the new rotary spray.
Said she, "Ah, that's better...
Why here's a French letter
That's been missing since Armistice Day!"

1941.

944

A lazy young lady named May
Was a torrid but troublesome lay.
    She was prone to conceive,
    So made haste to achieve
A bed with a built-in Bidet.

1943A.

945

Said a girl to her friend from Milpitas,
"There's a doctor in town who will treat us
    For feminine ills
    And hot and cold chills,
Or even abort a young fœtus."

1945.

946

There once was an innocent miss
Who feared she'd conceived from a kiss.
    So, as a precaution,
    She had an abortion,
But naught was forthcoming but piss.

1941.

947

There was a young girl from New York
Who expected a call from the stork.
    So with infinite caution
    She performed an abortion
With an icepick, a spoon, and a fork.

1941.

948

There was a young man, Mussolini,
Who found he had seven bambini.
    He said, "If I thought
    That the griddle was hot,
I'd never have put in the weenie!"

1946B.

949

There was a young lady named Myrtle
Whose womb was exceedingly fertile.
  Her pa got contortions
  At all her abortions,
And bought her a chastity girdle.

1944A.

950

Said a young man of Novorossisk,
"I use vulcanization by Fisk.
  Of course it comes higher,
  But when it's time to retire
You can frisk with a minimal risk."

1951.

951

There was a young fellow named Oram,
A model of tact and decorum.
  When about to fuck Grishkin
  He pulled out a fishskin
From the leaves of the Keats variorum.

1942.

952

There was a young man of Penzance
Who rogered his three maiden aunts.
  Though them he defiled,
  He ne'er got them with child,
Through using the letters of France.

1870.

953

There was a young girl from Penzance
Who decided to take just one chance.
  So she let herself go
  In the lap of her beau,
And now all her sisters are aunts.

1941.

954

In Spring Miss May marries Perce,
'Til then their pash' they disburse:
With a thin piece of rubber
There's no need to scrub 'er—
Of course, there's no harm to rehearse.

1927.

955

There was a young fellow named Peter
Who was laying his gal with a cheater,
When the rubber thing broke
And started to smoke
From the friction with her piss-hole (ureter).

1946A.

956. SOCIALLY CONSCIOUS PORNOGRAPHY

We've socially conscious biography,
Esthetics, and social geography.
Today every field
Boasts its Marxian yield,
So now there's class-conscious pornography.

Oh, the worker is nobody's fool,
For by rights he's the man with the tool.
His ponderous prick'll
Arise with the sickle,
And bugger the Fascists who rule.

Miss de Vaughan was a maker of panties
For all girls from subdebs to grand-aunties.
Her very best ad
Was herself, lightly clad
In her three-ninety-five silken scanties.

So this wench is a capitalist,
She's our villain and ought to be hissed.
    But she's lush and she's plump,
    And a glimpse of her rump
Would teach Marx that there's something he's missed.

Now de Vaughan had resolved on a lock-out
To give Communist Labor the knock-out.
    She said, "Fuck the foul fools."
    (She'd attended good schools),
And took a fresh bottle of Hock out.

Joseph Smith was a sturdy longshoreman
(And an eminent amateur whoreman).
    Just to be sympathetic
    He grew peripatetic,
'Til his picketing irked de Vaughan's doorman.

For this lout was a scab born and bred,
Who fainted whene'er he saw red:
    In distress he reported,
    But she only retorted,
"Run home and hide under your bed."

For her plans were peculiar and wicked,
As she thought, "He's a man, if a picket."
    She lured him inside
    And insidiously plied
The prick of the picket to lick it.

Joe's rod was as stiff as a rail,
But he couldn't let principles fail.
"You degenerate bitch,
That's a trick of the rich;
But the People prefer honest tail.

"You may tickle the cocks and the vanities
Of the rich men who purchase your scanities,
But the proud People's Front
Calls for sound hairy cunt.
So it's *down* with de Vaughan's panty-wanities."

He picked a soft couch in her office,
And tore off her pants and ripped off his.
Then he showed her the rod
Marks the difference, by God,
Between what a man and a toff is.

Now our Joe was the first proletarian
Who had filled with his sperm the ovarian
Recess of de Vaughan,
Which had sheltered the spawn
Of unnumbered Fascists, all Aryan.

Next day his friends said, "You've been soaring
You're dead on your feet. Were you whoring?"
He replied, "Starving masses
Mean more than plump asses.
Last night from within I was boring."

And de Vaughan thought her troubles were over,
Her picket had left (to recover),
    But he'd furnished her womb
    With incipient bloom :
A fact she had yet to discover.

So after nine months, to the day,
The employer in labor pains lay.
    As the boy hove in sight
    He yelled, " WORKERS UNITE! "
And the doctors all fainted away.

The moral of this is, my child,
By rich promises don't be beguiled.
    Remember that workers
    Are eminent firkers,
And go left, if you must be defiled.

1943A.

972

A grey-headed tutor named Porson
From some strange amatory contortion
    Believed he'd conceived
    A book, but relieved
Himself by a pamphlet abortion.

1942A.

973

Young girls of seductive proportions
Should take contraceptive precautions :
    Silly young Ermintrude
    Let one small sperm intrude...
Who's the best man for abortions?

1938.

974

A cautions young husband named Rafe
Used to diddle his wife with a safe.
Thus he thwarted God's wishes
And fed his pet fishes,
Which he kept in a bedside carafe.

1941.

975

There was a young man from Rangoon
Who was born at least three months too soon.
He hadn't the luck
To be born of a fuck,
But was shoveled in cold on a spoon.

1938-1947B.

976

Said a pregnant young lady named Sally,
"I've learned that it's consummate folly
To walk home from a dance
Without any pants
When the way home leads over the Pali."

1946.

977

There was a young girl of Samoa
Who plugged up her cunt with a boa.
This strange contraceptive
Was very deceptive
To all but the spermatozoa.

1941.

978

There was a young lady named Sharkey
Who had an affair with a darkey.
The result of her sins
Was quadruplets, not twins,
One white, and one black, and two khaki.

1927*-1943C.

979

A certain young man of St. Paul
Consistently practiced withdrawal.
    This quaint predilection
    Creation such friction,
He soon had no foreskin at all.

Withdrawal, according to Freud,
Is a very good thing to avoid.
    If practiced each day,
    Your balls will decay
To the size of a small adenoid.

Freud's opinion, said old Dr. Stekel,
Isn't worth a Confederate shekel.
    Withdrawal is fun—
    But beware lest the sun
Should cause the withdrawn parts to freckle.

1948A.

982

There was a young lady named Sheba,
Fell in love with an eager amoeba.
    This queer bit of jelly
    Crept into her belly,
And ecstatically murmured, "*Ich liebe!*"

1941.

983

Pity the spermatozoa!
His life leads him lower and lower.
    With fear in his belly
    He swims through the jelly,
But seldom increases the scoah.

1941.

984

A fearless young spermatozoa
Remarked to an ovum, " Helloa!
We'd make a cute fœtus,
But I fear she'd mistreat us—
By the smell of this place, she's a whoah. "

1941.

985

There once was a lady who'd sinned,
Who said as her abdomen thinned,
" By my unsullied honor,
I'm *not* a madonna!
My baby has gone with the wind. "

1947B.

986

A husband who craved to be sterile
Because of the pregnancy peril
Said, " I've thought of vasectomy,
But my wife then might hector me,
And threaten divorce when we quarrel. "

1941.

987

There was a young lady of Wantage
Of whom the Town Clerk took advantage.
Said the County Surveyor,
" Of course you must pay her;
You've altered the line of her frontage. "

1932.

988

There was an old codger named Wright
Who did nasty things just for spite.
He knocked up his daughter
And then tried to abort her
By biting her tits in the night.

1941.

XII

PROSTITUTION

989

There once was a girl from Alaska
Who would fuck whenever you'd ask her.
    But soon she grew nice
    And went up in price,
And no one could touch her but Jesus H. Christ,
Or possibly John Jacob Astor.

1927-1932.

990

A vicious old whore of Albania
Hated men with a terrible mania.
    With a twitch and a squirm
    She would hold back your sperm,
And then roll on her face and disdain ya.

1941.

991

There was an old whore of Algiers
Who had bushels of dirt in her ears.
    The tip of her titty
    Was also quite shitty,
She never had washed it in years.

1938-1941.

992

A guy met a girl in Anacostia.
And said, " Darling, dare I accost ya?
    I got only a buck,
    Is that good for a fuck?"
She replied, " Not a fart will it cost ya."

1943.

993

There once was a floozie named Annie
Whose prices were cosy—but canny:
A buck for a fuck,
Fifty cents for a suck,
And a dime for a feel of her fanny.

1943B.

994

Said an elderly whore named Arlene,
"I prefer a young lad of eighteen.
There's more cream in his larder,
And his pecker gets harder,
And he fucks in a manner obscene."

1942.

995

When the Duchess of Bagliofuente
Took her fourteenth *cavaliere servente*,
The Duke said, "Old chappy,
I'll keep that quim happy
If I have to hire nineteen or twenty."

1942A.

996

There was a young man from Berlin,
A patron of sexual sin,
He crammed the small crease
'Twixt the legs of his niece
With a foot of his old rolling pin.

1945.

997

There was a young chip from Brazil
Who fucked like a veritable mill.
There was never a whore,
When she'd finished her chore,
More prompt to present you her bill.

1942.

998

There was a young trucker named Briard
Who had a young whore that he hired
To fuck when not trucking,
But trucking *plus* fucking
Got him so fucking tired he got fired.

1941.

999

There was a young fellow called Cary,
Who got fucking the Virgin Mary.
And Christ was so bored
At seeing Ma whored
That he set himself up as a fairy.

1928.

1000

There once was a girl from the chorus
Whose virtue was known to be porous.
She started by candling,
And ended by handling
The whole clientèle of a whorehouse.

1943B.

1001

A hard-working waitress named Cora
Discovered that drummers adore a
Titty that's ripe
And a cunt that is tripe—
Now she doesn't work hard any more-a!

1941.

1002

A lady named Belle da Cunt Corrigan
Was the mistress of J. Pierpont Morigan,
Till she handed the banker
A hell of a chancre,
And now she is just a plain whore again.

1941.

1003

There was a young harlot of Crete
Whose fucking was far, far too fleet.
So they tied down her ass
With a long ton of brass
To give them a much longer treat.

When the Nazis landed in Crete
This young harlot had to compete
With the many Storm Troopers
Who were using their poopers
For other things than to excrete.

Our subversive young harlot of Crete
Was led to fifth-column deceit.
When the paratroops landed
Her trade she expanded
By at once going down on their meat.

Then here was this harlot of Crete,
She decided to be very neat.
She said, "I'm too high class
To ream common ass,
And I'll wash every prick that I eat."

And at last this fine harlot of Crete
Was hawking her meat in the street.
Ambling out one fine day
In a casual way,
She clapped up the whole British fleet.

1943-1951.

1008

There was a young lady from Cue
Who filled her vagina with glue.
She said with a grin,
"If they pay to get in,
They'll pay to get out of it too."

1947B.

1009

There was a young girl named Dale
Who put up her ass for sale.
For the sum of two bits
You could tickle her tits,
But a buck would get you real tail.

1942.

1010

To succeed in the brothels at Derna
One always begins as a learner.
Indentured at six
As a greaser of pricks,
One may rise to be fitter and turner.

1946B.

1011

There was a young girl from Des Moines
Who had a large sack full of coins.
The nickels and dimes
She got from the times
That she cradled the boys in her loins.

1945.

1012

A passion-swept dame called Dolores
Is the hottest of history's whores.
Though we fuck her with zest,
When we crawl home to rest,
Guess who's there waiting for us—
Dolores, of cour-es!

1941.

1013

A young man, quite free with his dong,
Said the thing could be had for a song.
Such response did he get
That he rented the Met,
And held auditions all the day long.

1942.

1014

A sempstress at Epping-on-Tyne
Used to peddle her tail down the line.
She first got a crown,
But her prices went down—
Now she'll fit you for ten pence or nine.

1942A.

1015

There was a young lady of Erskine,
And the chief of her charms was her fair skin,
But the sable she wore
(She had several more)
She had earned while wearing her bare skin.

1941.

1016

Two young girls who lived in Ft. Tunney
Decided to shop their dofunny.
" We had papa tutor us
To cash in on our uterus;
We park transients now, in each cunny! "

1943B.

1017

Said the whore whom they called Geraldine,
" When I think of the pricks that I've seen,
And all of the nuts
And the ass-holes and butts,
And the bastards like you in between... "

1942-1952.

1018

A notorious whore named Miss Hearst
In the weakness of men is well versed.
    Reads a sign o'er the head
    Of her well-rumpled bed:
"The customer always comes first."

1945.

1019

Said a pretty young whore of Hong Kong
To a long-pronged patron named Wong,
  "They say my vagina's
    The nicest in China—
Don't ruin it by donging it wrong."

1941.

1020

There was a young man of Jaipur
Whose cock was shot off in the War.
    So he painted the front
    To resemble a cunt,
And set himself up as a whore.

1938.

1021

Since donning a uniform, Joe
Quit the floozies that he used to know.
    Says he, "Joan Bennett'll
    Tickle my genital
Every night at the old U.S.O."

1944.

1022

A shiftless young fellow of Kent
Had his wife fuck the landlord for rent,
    But as she grew older
    The landlord grew colder,
And now they live out in a tent.

1941.

1023

There was an old girl of Kilkenny
Whose usual charge was a penny.
For the half of that sum
You could finger her bum—
A source of amusement to many.

1928-1947B.

1024

Said a madam named Mamie La Farge
To a sailor just off of a barge,
"We have one girl that's dead,
With a hole in her head—
Of course there's a slight extra charge."

1944A.

1025

Have you heard about Dorothy Lamour,
Whose lovers got fewer and fewer?
When asked why she lost 'em
She said, "I defrost 'em—
I guess I'm not made for a whore."

1942-1952.

1026

In the city of York there's a lass
Who will hitch up her dress when you pass.
If you toss her two bits
She will strip to the tits,
And let you explore her bare ass.

1945.

1027

A harlot of note named Le Dux
Would always charge seventy bucks.
But for that she would suck you,
And wink-off and fuck you—
The whole thing was simply de luxe!

1941.

1028

There was an old hag named Le Sueur
Who just was an out-and-out whore.
    Between her big teats
    You could come for two bits,
And she'd fuck in any old sewer.

1946A.

1029

Any whore whose door sports a red light
Knows a prick when she sees one, all right.
    She can tell by a glance
    At the drape of men's pants
If they're worth taking on for the night.

1943.

1030

There was a young lady named Mable
Who would fuck on a bed or a table.
    Though a two-dollar screw
    Was the best she could do,
Her ass bore a ten-dollar label.

1944-1952.

1031

There was a young whore from Madrid
Who anyone could fuck for a quid.
    But a bastard Italian
    With balls like a stallion
Said he'd do it for nothing—and did.

1938.

1032

Les cocottes de la ville de Marseille
Sont brunettes de l'ardent soleil.
    Elles pissent du vin blanc,
    Couchent pour dix francs —
Mais où sont les patentes de santé?

1942A.

1033

The tarts in the town of Marseilles
Are brunette from the sun every day.
    White wine is their piddle,
    For ten francs they'll diddle—
But their tickets of health, where are they?

1942A.

1034

Unique is a strumpet of Mazur
In the way that her clientèle pays her:
    A machine that she uses
    Clamps on to her whoosis,
And clocks everybody that lays her.

1941.

1035

There was an old whore named McGee
Who was just the right sort for a spree.
    She said, "For a fuck
    I charge half a buck,
And I throw in the ass-hole for free."

1944A.

1036

Said a dainty young whore named Miss Meggs,
"The men like to spread my two legs,
    Then slip in between,
    If you know what I mean,
And leave me the white of their eggs."

1943.

1037

Said a naked young soldier named Mickey
As his cunt eyed his stiff, throbbing dickey,
    "Kid, my leave's almost up,
    But I feel like a tup;
Bend down, and I'll slip you a quickie."

1951.

1038

A school marm from old Mississippi
Had a quim that was simply zippy.
The scholars all praised it
Till finally she raised it
To prices befitting a chippy.

1952.

1039

There was a young thing from Missouri
Who fancied herself as a houri.
Her friends thus forsook her,
For a harlot they took her,
And she gave up the role in a fury.

1952.

1040

There was a young lady named Moore
Who, while not quite precisely a whore,
Couldn't pass up a chance
To take down her pants,
And compare some man's stroke with her bore.

1941.

1041

A tired young trollop of Nome
Was worn out from her toes to her dome.
Eight miners came screwing,
But she said, "Nothing doing;
One of you has to go home!"

1941.

1042

There was a young woman of Norway
Who drove a rare trade in the whore way,
Till a sodomite Viscount
Brought cunt to a discount,
And the bawdy house belles to a poor way.

1870*

1043

Said Clark Gable, picking his nose,
"I get more than the public suppose.
Take the Hollywood way,
It's the women who pay,
And the men simply take off their clothes."

1939A.

1044

A chippy whose name was O'Dare
Sailed on a ship to Kenmare,
But this cute little honey
Had left home her money
So she laid the whole crew for her fare.

1946A.

1045

A sailor ashore in Peru
Said, "Signora, quanto por la screw?"
"For only one peso
I will, if you say so,
Be buggered and nibble it too."

1942A.

1046

A sprightly young tart in Pompeii
Used to make fifty drachma per lay.
But age dimmed her renown
And now she lies down
Fifty times for the same pay.

1942A.

1047

A soi-disant Mynheer Professor
Met a beat-up old whore from Odessa.
She applied all her arts
To his genital parts,
But they only grew lesser and lesser.

1948A.

1048

Says a busy young whore named Miss Randalls,
As men by the dozens she handles,
"When I get this busy
My cunt gets all jizzy,
And it runs down my legs like wax candles."

1942.

1049

A whorehouse at 9 rue de Rennes
Had trouble in luring in men,
Till they got some fairies
With pretty dillberries,
And their clientèle came back again.

1942A.

1050

There was a young lady in Reno
Who lost all her dough playing keeno.
But she lay on her back
And opened her crack,
And now she owns the casino.

1942.

1051

A prosperous merchant of Rhône
Took orders for cunt on the phone,
Or the same could be baled,
Stamped, labeled, and mailed
To a limited parcel-post zone.

DuPont, I. G., Monsanto, and Shell
Built a world-circling pussy cartel,
And by planned obsolescence
So controlled detumescence
A poor man could not get a smell.

1948A.

1053

There was a rich old roué
Who felt himself slipping away.
He endowed a large ward
In a house where he'd whored.
Was there a crowd at his funeral? I'll say!

1948.

1054

There was a hot girl from the Saar
Who fucked all, both from near and from far.
When asked to explain,
She replied with disdain,
" I'm trying to buy me a car. "

1943.

1055

There was a young girl from St. Cyr
Whose reflex reactions were queer.
Her escort said, " Mable,
Get up off the table;
That money's to pay for the beer. "

1949.

1056

A licentious old justice of Salem
Used to catch all the harlots and jail 'em.
But instead of a fine
He would stand them in line,
With his common-law tool to impale 'em.

1941.

1057

There was an old girl of Silesia
Who said, " As my cunt doesn't please ya,
You might as well come
Up my slimy old bum,
But be careful my tapeworm don't seize ya. "

1927-1941.

1058

Ethnologists up with the Sioux
Wired home for two punts, one canoe.
The answer next day
Said, " Girls on the way,
But what the hell's a 'panoe'? "

1946A.

1059

There was a young lady from Slough
Who said that she didn't know how.
Then a young fellow caught her
And jolly well taught her;
She lodges in Pimlico now.

1928.

1060

Said a girl from Staraya Russa,
Whom the war had made looser and looser,
" Yes, I'm wormin' a German,
A vermin named Hermann,
But his dink is a lollapalooza! "

1942.

1061

There was an old Count of Swoboda
Who would not pay a whore what he owed her.
So with great *savoir-faire*
She stood on a chair,
And pissed in his whiskey-and-soda.

1938-1941.

1062

There was an old man of Tagore
Who tried out his cook as a whore
He used Bridget's twidget
To fidget his digit,
And now she won't cook any more.

1941.

1063

There was a young whore from Tashkent
Who managed an immoral tent.
Day out and day in
She lay writhing in sin,
Giving thanks it was ten months to Lent.

1946B.

1064

A young girl who was no good at tennis,
But at swimming was really a menace,
Took pains to explain,
" It depends how you train :
I was a street-walker in Venice. "

1946.

1065

There was a young man from the War Office
Who got into bed with a whore of his.
She took off her drawers
With many a pause,
But the chap from the War Office tore off his.

1938.

1066

There was an old whore of Warsaw
Who fucked all her customers raw.
She would thump with her rump,
And punt with her cunt,
And lick every prick that she saw.

1941.

1067

There once was a knowledgeful whore
Who knew all the coital lore.
But she found there were many
Who preferred her fat fanny,
And now she don't fuck any more.

1948A.

1068

There once was a versatile whore,
As expert behind as before.
    For a quid you could view her,
    And bugger and screw her,
As she stood on her head on the floor.

1941.

1069

There was an old harlot of Wick
Who was sucking a coal-heaver's prick.
    She said, " I don't mind
    The coal-dust and grime,
But the smell of your balls makes me sick. "

1882-1941.

1070

There once was a harlot at Yale
With her price-list tattooed on her tail,
    And on her behind,
    For the sake of the blind,
She had it embroidered in Braille.

1941.

XIII

DISEASES

1071

Remember those two of Aberystwyth
Who connected the things that they pissed with?
  She sat on his lap
  But they both had the clap,
And they cursed with the things that they kissed
  with. 1928B-1944A.

1072

A sultan named Abou ben Adhem
Thus cautioned a travelling madam,
  "I suffer from crabs
  As do most us A-rabs,"
"It's alright," said the madam, "I've had
  'em." 1946A.

1073

There was an old whore of Azores
Whose cunt was all covered with sores.
  The dogs in the street
  Wouldn't eat the green meat
That hung in festoons from her drawers.
1941.

1074

There was a young fellow—a banker,
Had bubo, itch, pox, and chancre.
  He got all the four
  From a dirty old whore,
So he wrote her a letter to thank her.
1911-1927.

1075. LUETIC LAMENT

There was a young man of Back Bay
Who thought syphilis just went away,
    And felt that a chancre
    Was merely a canker
Acquired in lascivious play.

Now first he got acne vulgaris,
The kind that is rampant in Paris,
    It covered his skin,
    From forehead to shin,
And now people ask where his hair is.

With symptoms increasing in number,
His aorta's in need of a plumber,
    His heart is cavorting,
    His wife is aborting,
And now he's acquired a gumma.

Consider his terrible plight—
His eyes won't react to the light,
    His hands are apraxic,
    His gait is ataxic,
He's developing gun-barrel sight.

His passions are strong, as before,
But his penis is flaccid, and sore,
    His wife now has tabes
    And sabre-shinned babies—
She's really worse off than a whore.

There are pains in his belly and knees,
His sphincters have gone by degrees,
Paroxysmal incontinence,
With all its concomitants,
Brings on quite unpredictable pees.

Though treated in every known way,
His spirochetes grow day by day,
He's developed paresis,
Converses with Jesus,
And thinks he's the Queen of the May.

1938-1941.

1082

There was a young girl of Bavaria
Who thought her disease was malaria.
But the family doc
Remarked to her shock,
"It is in the mercurial area."

1941.

1083

A noble young lord named Bellasis
Was a sad case of satyriasis,
Till help psychiatric
Brought the fucking fanatic
To a state of sexual stasis.

1947B.

1084

There was a young man of Berlin
Whom disease had despoiled of his skin,
But he said with much pride,
"Though deprived of my hide,
I can still enjoy a put in."

1879.

1085

There was a young man of Cashmere
Who purchased a fine Bayadere.
He fucked all her toes,
Her mouth, eyes, and her nose,
And eventually poxed her left ear.

1879.

1086

There was a young woman of Cheadle
Who once gave the clap to a beadle.
Said she, "Does it itch?"
"It does, you damned bitch,
And burns like hell-fire when I peedle."

1879.

1087

There was a young woman of Chester
Who said to the man who undressed her,
"I think you will find
That it's better behind—
The front is beginning to fester.

1927-1941.

1088

There was an old sarge of Dorchester
Who invented a mechanical whore-tester.
With an electrical eye,
His tool, and a die,
He observed each sore pimple and fester.

1944.

1089

There's a man in the city of Dublin
Whose pego is always him troubling,
And it's now come to this,
That he can't go to piss,
But the spunk with the piddle comes bubbling.

1870.

1090

There was a young priest of Dundee
Who went back of the parish to pee.
He said, " *Pax vobiscum,*
Why doesn't the piss come?
I must have the c-l-a-p. "

1928*-1941.

1091

There was an old party of Fife
Who suspected a clap in his wife.
So he bought an injection
To cure the infection,
Which gave him a stricture for life.

1870.

1092

There was a young rounder named Fisk
Whose method of screwing was brisk.
And his reason was : " If
The damned bitch has the syph,
This way I'm reducing the risk. "

1941.

1093

A horny young soldier named Frank
Had only his girl-friend to thank
That he didn't catch clap,
Gonorrhea or pap,
And wind up in an oxygen tank.

1943.

1094

A president called Gambetta
Once used an imperfect French Letter.
This was not the worst,
With disease he got cursed,
And he took a long time to get better.

1879.

1095

There was a young lady of Gaza
Who shaved her cunt clean with a razor.
The crabs in a lump
Made tracks to her rump,
Which proceeding did greatly amaze her.

1879.

1096

There was an old man of Goditch,
Had the syph and the clap and the itch.
His name was McNabs
And he also had crabs,
The dirty old son of a bitch.

1927-1941.

1097

There was a young lady from Ipswich
Who had syphilis, pox, and the itch.
In her box she put pepper
And slept with a leper,
And ruined that son of a bitch.

1945C.

1098

A lecherous fellow named Gould
Soliloquized thus to his tool:
"From Cape Cod to Salamanca,
You've had pox, clap, and chancre—
Now ain't you a bloody great fool?"

1939A-1946B.

1099

There was a young lady of Grotton
Had to plug up her coosie with cotton,
For it was no myth
That the girl had the syph—
She stunk, and her titties were rotten.

1941.

1100

There was a young woman of Hadley
Who would with an omnibus cad lie.
He gave her the crabs,
And besides minor scabs
The pox too she got very badly.

1870.

1101

A strapping young fellow named Herman
Had a ring round his prick that was permanent.
All the old docs
Said the ring was the pox,
But he swore it was lipstick or vermin.

1941.

1102

There was a young lady named Hitchin
Who was scratching her crotch in the kitchen.
Her mother said, " Rose,
It's the crabs, I suppose. "
She said, " Yes, and the buggers are itchin'. "

1879-1941.

1103

Young Tom Doane, a promising jockey,
Laid up his spurs, feeling rocky.
" I have got saddle-galls
On both of my balls. "
But the doctor wrote down : Gonococci.

1942A.

1104

There was a young girl of Kilkenny
On whose genital parts there were many
Venereal growths—
The result of wild oats
Sown there by a fellow named Benny.

1946A.

1105

There was a young maid of Klepper
Went out one night with a stepper,
    And now in dismay
    She murmurs each day,
" His pee-pee was made of red-pepper! "

1927.

1106

The physicians of Countess van Krapp
Found a terrible rash on her map—
    Sores that opened and closed
    Which they soon diagnosed
As a case of perennial clap.

1941.

1107

There was a young lady named Lea
Whose favors were frequent and free,
    And pants-pigeons flew
    Where her goose-berries grew,
And some of them flew onto me.

1944A.

1108

He'll be there to inspect me,
With a big syringe to inject me—
    Oh, I'll be humpbacked
    Before I get back
To Ten-Ten-Tennessee...

1919-1939*

1109

There was a young lady of Michigan
Who said, " Damn it! I've got the itch again. "
    Said her mother, " That's strange,
    I'm surprised it ain't mange,
If you've slept with that son-of-a-bitch again. "

1941.

1110

There was an old man of Molucca
Who wanted his daughter, to fuck her.
But she got the best
Of his little incest,
And poxed the old man of Molucca.

1870.

1111

There was a young lady named Nance
Who had ants in the seat of her pants.
When they bit her on bottom
She yelled, " Jesus God rot 'em!
I can't do the St. Vitus dance. "

1942-1952.

1112

There once was a Spanish nobilio
Who lived in a Spanish castilio,
His *cojones* grew hot
Much more often than not,
At the thought of a Spanish jazzilio.

1941*

1113

The wife of a Viking in Norway
Was caught taking a nap in a doorway.
" When you make the attack,
Let it be from the back,
Because lately the front way's the sore way. "

1942A.

1114

Alack, for the doughty O'Connor
Who fucked like a fiend for his honor,
Till a flapper named Rhea
Colluded to be a
Mother to Leuco and Gonor.

1942A.

1115

A charming young lady named Randall
Has a clap that the doctors can't handle.
So this lovely, lorn floozie,
With her poor, damaged coosie,
Must take her delight with a candle.

1941.

1116

A rank whore, there ne'er was a ranker,
Possessed an Hunterian chancre,
But she made an elision
By a transverse incision,
For which all her lovers may thank her.

1870.

1117

There was a young lady of Reading,
Who got poxed, and the virus kept spreading.
Her nymphae each day
Kept sloughing away,
Till at last you could shove your whole head in.

1882.

1118

A girl to the druggist did say,
" I am bothered with bugs in my hay. "
" I see what you mean,
You need Paris green
To be rid of the things right away. "

The results of this piece of mischance
Were disastrous, you'll see at a glance.
First died bugs, then went trees,
Then her pet Pekinese,
And two gentlemen just in from France.

1948A.

1120

There was a young lady at sea
Who said, " God, how it hurts me to pee. "
" I see, " said the mate,
" That accounts for the state
Of the captain, the purser, and me. "

1925*-1927.

1121

A virile young G.I. named Shorty
Was lively, and known to be " sporty. "
But he once made a slip
And showed up with a " drip, "
And was red-lined (35-1440).

1943.

1122

A boy whose skin long I suppose is,
Was dreadfully ill with phymosis.
The doctor said, " Why,
Circumcision we'll try,
A plan recommended by Moses. "

1870.

1123

There was an old man of Tantivy
Who followed his son to the privy.
He lifted the lid
To see what he did,
And found that it smelt of Capivi.

1879.

1124

There was an old man at the Terminus
Whose bush and whose bum were all verminous.
They said, " You *sale Boche!*
You really must wash
Before you start planting your sperm in us. "

1928.

1125

There was a young girl of Uttoxeter,
And all the young men shook their cocks at her.
From one of these cocks
She contracted the pox,
And she poxed all the cocks in Uttoxeter.

1870-1941.

1126

A fellow who slept with a whore
Used a safe, but his pecker got sore.
Said he with chagrin,
" Selling these is a sin. "
Said the druggist, " *Caveat emptor.* "

1946.

1127

Full ninety years old was friend Wynn
When he went to a hookshop to sin.
But try as he would
It did him no good.
For all he had left was the skin.

1927-1948.

1128

There was a young lady of Yap
Who had pimples all over her map.
But in her interstices
There lurked a far worse disease,
Commonly known as the clap.

1947B.

XIV

LOSSES

NOTE

[*Losses through the agency of animals*
will be found in Chapter VII, " Zoophily."

Losses in connection with masturbation
will be found in Chapter XV, " Sex Substitutes."]

1129

There was a young lady of Alnwicke
Whom a stranger threw into a panic.
  For he frigged her and fucked her,
  And buggered and sucked her,
With a glee hardly short of satanic.

1941.

1130

I lost my arm in the army,
I lost my leg in the navy,
  I lost my balls
  Over Niagara Falls,
And I lost my cock in a lady.

1939*

1131

An explorer returned from Australia,
Reported lost paraphernalia :
  A Zeiss microscope
  And his personal hope,
Which had vanished with his genitalia.

1942A.

1132

There was a young sailor named Bates
Who did the fandango on skates.
He fell on his cutlass
Which rendered him nutless
And practically useless on dates.

1944-1952.

1133

There was an old maid from Bermuda
Who shot a marauding intruder.
It was not her ire
At his lack of attire,
But he reached for her jewels as he screwed her.

1950.

1134

There was a young fellow named Bill
Who took an atomic pill.
His navel corroded,
His asshole exploded,
And they found his nuts in Brazil.

1948.

1135

While pissing on deck, an old boatswain
Fell asleep, and his pisser got frozen.
It snapped at the shank,
And it fell off and sank
In the sea—'twas his own fault for dozin'.

1941.

1136

There was a young fellow named Bob
Who explained to his friends with a sob,
"The size of my phallus
Was just right for Alice
Till the night that she bit off the knob."

1941.